Collected Poems

ELIZABETH JENNINGS

Collected Poems
1953-1985

First published in 1986
First published in paperback in 1987 by
CARCANET PRESS LIMITED
208-212 Corn Exchange, Manchester M4 3BQ, UK

and 198 Sixth Avenue, New York
NY10013

British Library Cataloguing in Publication Data

Jennings, Elizabeth
  Collected poems.
  I. Title
  821'.914   PR6060.E1

ISBN 0-85635-648-4 H/B
ISBN 0-85635-721-9 P/B

The Publisher acknowledges the financial assistance of
the Arts Council of Great Britain

Typeset by Bryan Williamson, Swinton, Berwickshire
Printed in England by SRP Ltd., Exeter

for Roy Fuller

Contents

5

from *Song for a Birth or a Death* (1961)

from *Consequently I Rejoice* (1977)

11

PREFACE

IN assembling this volume of *Collected Poems* I have drawn on sixteen earlier books including some of my translations of Michelangelo's *Sonnets* and a book which, I believe, may truly be called "for children of all ages", *After The Ark*. An early *Collected Poems* of mine appeared in 1967 and I have, of course, used this as my starting-point though I have included a few more of my early poems in this volume. The index indicates from which of my books of verse all the poems represented here have come. Since 1967 nine more books of poems have appeared. This book, however, is not a *Complete Poems*. It contains all the work which I still hope is worth preserving from my first book *Poems* (1953) to *Extending the Territory* which came out in 1985. I have discarded work rather than re-written whole poems or parts of them. It is my belief that an early poem, if it has any value, should, when collected, be left as it is. My method of writing poems has always been to work through many drafts of whole poems until I have reached the one which seems to me to say what I want to say in the right words and form. The final draft thus comes out very cleanly, with little alteration.

When I re-read my past work I can see a development; to such an effect, indeed, that some of them seem no longer to be any part of me. But of course, once a poem is published it ceases to have much to do with oneself. Art is not self-expression while, for me, "confessional poetry" is almost a contradiction in terms.

Elizabeth Jennings

13

Delay

The radiance of that star that leans on me
Was shining years ago. The light that now
Glitters up there my eye may never see,
And so the time lag teases me with how

Love that loves now may not reach me until
Its first desire is spent. The star's impulse
Must wait for eyes to claim it beautiful
And love arrived may find us somewhere else.

Winter Love

Let us have winter loving that the heart
May be in peace and ready to partake
Of the slow pleasure spring would wish to hurry
Or that in summer harshly would awake,
And let us fall apart, O gladly weary,
The white skin shaken like a white snowflake.

Reminiscence

When I was happy alone, too young for love
Or to be loved in any but a way
Cloudless and gentle, I would find the day
Long as I wished its length or web to weave.

I did not know or could not know enough
To fret at thought or even try to whittle
A pattern from the shapeless stony stuff
That now confuses since I've grown too subtle.

I used the senses, did not seek to find
Something they could not touch, made numb with fear;
I felt the glittering landscape in the mind
And O was happy not to have it clear.

Fantasy

Tree without leaf I stand
Bird unfeathered cannot fly
I a beggar weep and cry
Not for coins but for a hand

To beg with. All my leaves are down,
Feathers flown and hand wrenched off
Bird and tree and beggar grown
Nothing on account of love.

Italian Light

It is not quite a house without the sun
And sun is what we notice, wonder at
As if stone left its hard and quarried state
To be reciprocal to light and let
The falling beams bound and rebound upon
Shutter and wall, each with assurance thrown.

So on descending from the snow we meet
Not warmth of south but houses which contrive
To be designed of sun. The builders have
Instructed hands to know where shadows fall
And made of buildings an obedient stone
Linked to the sun as waters to the moon.

Afternoon in Florence

This afternoon disturbs within the mind
No other afternoon, is out of time
Yet lies within a definite sun to end
In night that is in time. Yet hold it here
Our eyes, our minds, to make the city clear.

Light detains no prisoner here at all
In brick or stone but sends a freedom out
Extends a shadow like a deeper thought,
Makes churches move, once still,
Rocking in light as music rocks the bell,

So eyes make room for light and minds make room
For image of the city tangible.
We look down on the city and a dream
Opens to wakefulness, and waking on
This peace perpetuates this afternoon.

Identity

When I decide I shall assemble you
Or, more precisely, when I decide which thoughts
Of mine about you fit most easily together,
Then I can learn what I have loved, what lets
Light through the mind. The residue
Of what you may be goes. I gather

Only as lovers or friends gather at all
For making friends means this –
Image and passion combined into a whole
Pattern within the loving mind, not her or his
Concurring there. You can project the full
Picture of lover or friend that is not either.

So then assemble me,
Your exact picture firm and credible,
Though as I think myself I may be free
And accurate enough.
That you love what is truthful to your will
Is all that ever can be answered for
And, what is more,
Is all we make each other when we love.

The Idler

An idler holds that rose as always rose,
Will not, before the bud discloses it
Within a later season, in his thought
Unwrap the flower and force the petals open
And wish in mind a different rose to happen.

So will not colour it with his own shadow
As we contrive, living beyond the present,
To move all things away from their own moment
And state another time for us. O who
Watches may yet make time refuse to grow.

So has his subtle power wiser than ours
And need elaborate no peace at all.
Watch how a landscape kindest is to idlers
Helping their shiftlessness grow to new powers,
Composing stillness round their careless will.

Bell-Ringer

The bells renew the town, discover it
And give it back itself again, the man
Pulling the rope collects the houses as
Thoughts gather in the mind unscanned, he is
Crowding the town together from the night
And making bells the morning, in remote

Control of every life (for bells shout "Wake"
And shake out dreams, though it is he who pulls
The sleep aside). But not into his thought
Do men continue as in lives of power;

For when each bell is pulled sufficiently
He never sees himself as any cause
Or need; the sounds had left his hands to sing
A meaning for each listening separately,
A separate meaning for the single choice.

18

Yet bells retire to silence, need him when
Time must be shown a lucid interval
And men look up as if the air were full
Of birds descending, bells exclaiming in
His hands but shouting wider than his will.

The Climbers

To the cold peak without their careful women
(Who watching children climbing into dreams
Go dispossessed at home). The mountain moves
Away at every climb and steps are hard
Frozen along the glacier. Every man
Tied to the rope constructs himself alone.

And not the summit reached nor any pole
Touched is the wished embrace, but still to move
And as the mountain climbs to see it whole
And each mind's landscape growing more complete
As sinews strain and all the muscles knot.

One at the peak is small. His disappointment
The coloured flag flown at the lonely top,
And all the valley's motive grown obscure.
He envies the large toilers halfway there
Who still possess the mountain by desire
And, not arriving, dream in no resentment.

Fishermen

This to be peace, they think beside the river
Being adapted well to expectation
And their wives' mutiny at no achievement,
And yet can sit watching the promises
Escape through weeds and make a trial of biting,
Can lose them, thankful that it is not yet
Time to draw in the line and drain the net.

Learning themselves in this uncertainty
Each hardly cares whether a fish is caught,
For here is privacy, each warns himself,
The fish, inquiries in the river, not
When drawn out promises at all
Being so solid on the bank and still.

Only the boys who live in certainty,
With expectation other than the stream,
Jeer at the patience and draw up their net
Of future frogs, the river vague to them
Until it's emptied. But the old men fill
Their eyes with water, leave the river full.

The Island

All travellers escape the mainland here.
The same geology torn from the stretch
Of hostile homelands is a head of calm,
And the same sea that pounds a foreign beach
Turns strangers here familiar, looses them
Kindly as pebbles shuffled up the shore.

Each brings an island in his heart to square
With what he finds, and all is something strange
But most expected. In this innocent air
Thoughts can assume a meaning, island strength
Is outward, inward, each man measures it,
Unrolls his happiness a shining length.

And this awareness grows upon itself,
Fastens on minds, is forward, backward, here.
The island focuses escape and free
Men on the shore are also islands, steer
Self to knowledge of self in the calm sea,
Seekers who are their own discovery.

Poem in Winter

Today the children begin to hope for snow
And look in the sky for auguries of it.
It is not for such omens that we wait,
Our world may not be settled by the slow
Falling of flakes to lie across our thought.

And even if the snow comes down indeed
We still shall stand behind a pane of glass
Untouched by it, and watch the children press
Their image on the drifts the snow has laid
Upon a winter they think they have made.

This is a wise illusion. Better to
Believe the near world is created by
A wish, a shaping hand, a certain eye,
Than hide in the mind's corner as we do
As though there were no world, no fall of snow.

Song at the Beginning of Autumn

Now watch this autumn that arrives
In smells. All looks like summer still;
Colours are quite unchanged, the air
On green and white serenely thrives.
Heavy the trees with growth and full
The fields. Flowers flourish everywhere.

Proust who collected time within
A child's cake would understand
The ambiguity of this –
Summer still raging while a thin
Column of smoke stirs from the land
Proving that autumn gropes for us.

But every season is a kind
Of rich nostalgia. We give names –
Autumn and summer, winter, spring –

As though to unfasten from the mind
Our moods and give them outward forms.
We want the certain, solid thing.

But I am carried back against
My will into a childhood where
Autumn is bonfires, marbles, smoke;
I lean against my window fenced
From evocations in the air.
When I said autumn, autumn broke.

Kings

You send an image hurrying out of doors
When you depose a king and seize his throne:
You exile symbols when you take by force.

And even if you say the power's your own,
That you are your own hero, your own king
You will not wear the meaning of the crown.

The power a ruler has is how men bring
Their thoughts to bear upon him, how their minds
Construct the grandeur from the simple thing.

And kings prevented from their proper ends
Make a deep lack in men's imaginings;
Heroes are nothing without worshipping,

Will not diminish into lovers, friends.

The Enemies

Last night they came across the river and
Entered the city. Women were awake
With lights and food. They entertained the band,
Not asking what the men had come to take
Or what strange tongue they spoke
Or why they came so suddenly through the land.

Now in the morning all the town is filled
With stories of the swift and dark invasion;
The women say that not one stranger told
A reason for his coming. The intrusion
Was not for devastation:
Peace is apparent still on hearth and field.

Yet all the city is a haunted place.
Man meeting man speaks cautiously. Old friends
Close up the candid looks upon their face.
There is no warmth in hands accepting hands;
Each ponders, "Better hide myself in case
Those strangers have set up their homes in minds
I used to walk in. Better draw the blinds
Even if the strangers haunt in my own house."

In This Time

If the myth's outworn, the legend broken,
    Useless even within the child's story
Since he sees well they now bring light no longer
    Into our eyes: and if our past retreats
And blows away like dust along the desert,
    Not leading to our moment now at all,
Settling us in this place and saying "Here
    In you I shall continue" – then what kind
Of lives have we? Can we make myths revive
    By breathing on them? Is there any taper
That will return the glitter to our eyes?

We have retreated inward to our minds
    Too much, have made rooms there with all doors closed,
All windows shuttered. There we sit and mope
    The myth away, set by the lovely legends;
Hardly we hear the children shout outside.
    We only know a way to love ourselves,
Have lost the power that made us lose ourselves.
    O let the wind outside blow in again
And the dust come and all the children's voices.
    Let anything that is not us return.
Myths are the memories we have rejected
    And legends need the freedom of our minds.

23

Beyond Possession

Our images withdraw, the rose returns
To what it was before we looked at it.
We lift our looks from where the water runs
And it's pure river once again, we write
No emblems on the trees. A way begins
Of living where we have no need to beat
The petals down to get the scent of rose
Or sign our features where the water goes.

All is itself. Each man himself entire,
Not even plucking out his thought, not even
Bringing a tutored wilfulness to bear
Upon the rose, the water. Each has given
Essence of water back to itself, essence of flower,
Till he is yoked to his own heart and driven
Inward to find a private kind of peace
And not a mind reflecting his own face.

Yet must go deeper still, must move to love
Where thought is free to let the water ride,
Is liberal to the rose giving it life
And setting even its own shadow aside;
Till flower and water blend with freedom of
Passion that does not close them in and hide
Their deepest natures; but the heart is strong
To beat with rose and river in one song.

Tribute

Sometimes the tall poem leans across the page
And the whole world seems near, a simple thing.
Then all the arts of mind and hand engage
To make the shadow tangible. O white
As silence is the page where words shall sing
And all the shadows be drawn into light.

And no one else is necessary then.
The poem is enough that joins me to
The world that seems too far to grasp at when
Images fail and words are gabbled speech:
At those times clarity appears in you,
Your mind holds meanings that my mind can reach.

Are you remote, then, when words play their part
With a fine arrogance within the poem?
Will the words keep all else outside my heart,
Even you, my test of life and gauge?
No, for you are that place where poems find room,
The tall abundant shadow on my page.

Mirrors

Was it a mirror then across a room,
A crowded room of parties where the smoke
Rose to the ceiling with the talk? The glass
Stared back at me a half-familiar face
Yet something hoped for. When at last you came
It was as if the distant mirror spoke.

That loving ended as all self-love ends
And teaches us that only fair-grounds have
The right to show us halls of mirrors where
In every place we look we see our stare
Taunting our own identities. But love
Perceives without a mirror in the hands.

In the Night

Out of my window late at night I gape
And see the stars but do not watch them really,
And hear the trains but do not listen clearly;
Inside my mind I turn about to keep
Myself awake, yet am not there entirely.
Something of me is out in the dark landscape.

How much am I then what I think, how much what I feel?
How much the eye that seems to keep stars straight?
Do I control what I can contemplate
Or is it my vision that's amenable?
I turn in my mind, my mind is a room whose wall
I can see the top of but never completely scale.

All that I love is, like the night, outside,
Good to be gazed at, looking as if it could
With a simple gesture be brought inside my head
Or in my heart. But my thoughts about it divide
Me from my object. Now deep in my bed
I turn and the world turns on the other side.

Recapitulation

Being a child it was enough to stand
    The centre of a world and let success
Come crowding in, be taken by the hand.
This was one way to lose a loneliness.

Until success itself became a part
    I played. It was the shell and centre too.
My mind was somewhere else, also my heart.
    I could not tell the false self from the true.

Now I abandon all my attributes –
    Failure, success, despair – until I have
Nothing at all but hard invincible doubts
    Shaping the one self that I can believe.

Answers

I kept my answers small and kept them near;
Big questions bruised my mind but still I let
Small answers be a bulwark to my fear.

The huge abstractions I kept from the light;
Small things I handled and caressed and loved.
I let the stars assume the whole of night.

But the big answers clamoured to be moved
Into my life. Their great audacity
Shouted to be acknowledged and believed.

Even when all small answers build up to
Protection of my spirit, still I hear
Big answers striving for their overthrow

And all the great conclusions coming near.

The Child and the Shadow

Your shadow I have seen you play with often.
O and it seems a shadow light before you,
Glittering behind you. You can see what lies
Beneath its marking dappled on the water
        Or on the earth a footprint merely;
No total darkness is cast by your body.

Say that it is a game of identities this –
You chasing yourself not caring whatever you find.
You have not sought a use for mirrors yet,
It is not your own shadow that you watch,
        Only our world which you learn slowly:
Our shadows strive to mingle with your own,

Chase them, then, as you chase the leaves or a bird,
Disturb us, disturb us, still let the light lie gently
Under the place that you carve for yourself in air;
Look, the fish are darting beneath your reflection
        But you see deep beyond your glance:
It is our shadow that slides in between.

Old Woman

So much she caused she cannot now account for
As she stands watching day return, the cool
Walls of the house moving towards the sun.
She puts some flowers in a vase and thinks
    "There is not much I can arrange
In here and now, but flowers are suppliant

As children never were. And love is now
A flicker of memory, my body is
My own entirely. When I lie at night
I gather nothing now into my arms,
    No child or man, and where I live
Is what remains when men and children go."

Yet she owns more than residue of lives
That she has marked and altered. See how she
Warns time from too much touching her possessions
By keeping flowers fed, by polishing
    Her fine old silver. Gratefully
She sees her own glance printed on grandchildren.

Drawing the curtains back and opening windows
Every morning now, she feels her years
Grow less and less. Time puts no burden on
Her now she does not need to measure it.
    It is acceptance she arranges
And her own life she places in the vase.

Old Man

His age drawn out behind him to be watched:
It is his shadow you may say. That dark
He paints upon the wall is his past self,
A mark he only leaves when he is still
    And he is still now always,
At ease and watching all his life assemble.

And he intends nothing but watching. What
His life has made of him his shadow shows –
Fine graces gone but dignity remaining,
While all he shuffled after is composed
   Into a curve of dark, of silences:
An old man tranquil in his silences.

And we move round him, are his own world turning,
Spinning it seems to him, leaving no shadow
To blaze our trail. We are our actions only:
He is himself, abundant and assured,
   All action thrown away,
And time is slowing where his shadow stands.

Taken by Surprise

Before, the anticipation, the walk merely
Under the oaks, (the afternoon crushed down
To his pressed footprints), noon surrendered, forgotten –
And the man moving, singular under the sun
With the hazel held in his hand lightly, lightly:
On the edge of his ear the lisp of the wind among
Untrembling leaves. Sun at the tips of the trees
Looked down, looked cold, and the man felt easy there.
His shadow seemed fitting as never before it was,
And the almost silence a space a man may enter
And be forgotten by all but his secret thoughts.
Then, something taking his fingers: "Is it the wind?"
He thought and looked to see if the branches moved.
But nothing unusual stirred the trees, again
His fingers trembled, the hazel shook, he felt
Suddenly life in the twig as a woman feels
Abrupt and close the stir of the unborn child.
O and the afternoon was altered then;
Power from all quarters flung at him, silence broke
And deft but uneasy far at the back of his mind
A word like water shuddered, streams gushed and fountains
Rose as the hazel leapt from his mastered hand.

The Storm

Right in the middle of the storm it was.
So many winds were blowing none could tell
Which was the fiercest or if trees that bent
So smoothly to each impulse had been waiting
All of their growing-time for just that impulse
To prove how pliable they were. Beneath,
Beasts fled away through fern, and stiffest grasses,
Which bent like fluid things, made tidal motion.

These who had never met before but in
Calmest surroundings, found all shadows mingling;
No stance could be struck here, no peace attained,
And words blew round in broken syllables,
Half-meanings sounded out like trumpet blasts,
Decisive words were driven into hiding.
Yet some hilarity united them
And faces, carved and cleared by rain and lightning,
Stared out as if they never had been seen.

And children now, lost in the wood together,
Becoming the behaviour of the wind,
The way the light fell, learnt each other newly
And sudden gentleness was apprehended
Till the abating winds, the whole storm swerving
Into another quarter, left them standing
Unwild and watching in bewilderment
Their own delusive shadows slow and part.

Her Garden

Not at the full moon will she pick those flowers
For sudden shade indoors would make them wilt.
The petals would drop down on polished wood
Adding another element to decay
Which all her old rooms are infected with.

Only outside she can put off the course
Of her disease. She has the garden built
Within high walls so no one can intrude.
When people pass she only hears the way
Their footsteps sound, never their closer breath.

But in her borders she observes the powers
Of bud and branch, forgetting how she felt
When, blood within her veins like sap, she stood,
Her arms like branches bare above the day
And all the petals strewn along her path.

No matter now for she has bridged the pause
Between fruition and decay. She'll halt
A little in her garden while a mood
Of peace so fills her that she cannot say
Whether it is the flowers' life or her death.

Summer and Time

Now when the days descend
We do not let them lie
But ponder on the end,
How morning air drained dry
Of mist will but contend
Later with evening sky.

And so we mix up time.
Children, we say, ignore
Before and after, chime
Only the present hour.
But we are wrong, they climb
What time is aiming for

But beg no lastingness.
And it is we who try
In every hour to press
Befores and afters, sigh
All the great hour's success
And set the spoiling by.

Heavy the heat today,
Even the clocks seem slow.
But children make no play
With summers years ago.
It is we who betray
Who tease the sun-dial so.

At Noon

Lying upon my bed I see
Full moon at ease. Each way I look
A world established without me
Proclaims itself. I take a book
And flutter through the pages where
Sun leaps through shadows. And I stare

Straight through the words and find again
A world that has no need of me.
The poems stride against the strain
Of complex rhythms. Separately
I lie and struggle to become
More than a centre to this room.

I want the ease of noon outside
Also the strength of words which move
Against their music. All the wide
And casual day I need to stuff
With my own meaning and the book
Of poems reflect me where I look.

Ghosts

Those houses haunt in which we leave
Something undone. It is not those
Great words or silences of love

That spread their echoes through a place
And fill the locked-up unbreathed gloom.
Ghosts do not haunt with any face

That we have known; they only come
With arrogance to thrust at us
Our own omissions in a room.

The words we would not speak they use,
The deeds we dared not act they flaunt,
Our nervous silences they bruise;

It is our helplessness they choose
And our refusals that they haunt.

Absence

I visited the place where we last met.
Nothing was changed, the gardens were well-tended,
The fountains sprayed their usual steady jet;
There was no sign that anything had ended
And nothing to instruct me to forget.

The thoughtless birds that shook out of the trees,
Singing an ecstasy I could not share,
Played cunning in my thoughts. Surely in these
Pleasures there could not be a pain to bear
Or any discord shake the level breeze.

It was because the place was just the same
That made your absence seem a savage force,
For under all the gentleness there came
An earthquake tremor: fountain, birds and grass
Were shaken by my thinking of your name.

Disguises

Always we have believed
We can change overnight,
Put a different look on the face,
Old passions out of sight:

33

And find new days relieved
Of all that we regretted
But something always stays
And will not be outwitted.

Say we put on dark glasses,
Wear different clothes and walk
With a new unpractised stride –
Always somebody passes
Undeceived by disguises
Or the different way we talk.
And we who could have defied
Anything if it was strange
Have nowhere we can hide
From those who refuse to change.

The Parting

Though there was nothing final then,
No word or look or sign,
I felt some ending in the air
As when a sensed design
Draws back from the completing touch
And dies along a line.

For through the words that seemed to show
That we were learning each
Trick of the other's thought and sense,
A shyness seemed to reach
As if such talk continuing
Would make the hour too rich.

Maybe this strangeness only was
The safe place all men make
To hide themselves from happiness;
I only know I lack
The strangeness our last meeting had
And try to force it back.

Resemblances

Always I look for some reminding feature,
Compel a likeness where there is not one,
As in a gallery I trace the stature
Of that one's boldness or of this one's grace.
Yet likenesses so searched for will yield none;
One feature, yes, but never the whole face.

So every face falls back into its parts
And once-known glances leave the candid look
Of total strangeness. Where the likeness starts
We fix attention, set aside the rest,
As those who scan for notes a thick-packed book,
Recalling only what has pleased them best.

And doing this, so often I have missed
Some recognition never known before,
Some knowledge which I never could have guessed.
And how if all the others whom I pass
Should like myself be always searching for
The special features only one face has?

Always the dear enchanted moment stays.
We cannot unlearn all whom we have loved;
Who can tear off like calendars the days
Or wipe out features fixed within the mind?
Only there should be some way to be moved
Beyond the likeness to the look behind.

A Death

"His face shone" she said,
"Three days I had him in my house,
Three days before they took him from his bed,
And never have I felt so close."

"Always alive he was
A little drawn away from me.
Looks are opaque when living and his face
Seemed hiding something, carefully."

35

"But those three days before
They took his body out, I used to go
And talk to him. That shining from him bore
No secrets. Living, he never looked or answered so."

Sceptic, I listened, then
Noted what peace she seemed to have,
How tenderly she put flowers on his grave
But not as if he might return again
Or shine or seem quite close:
Rather to please us were the flowers she gave.

The Shot

The bullet shot me and I lay
So calm beneath the sun, the trees
Shook out their shadows in the breeze
Which carried half the sky away.

I did not know if I was dead,
A feeling close to sleep lay near
Yet through it I could see the clear
River and grass as if in bed

I lay and watched the morning come
Gentle behind the blowing stuff
Of curtains. But the pain was rough,
Not fitting to a sunlit room.

And I am dying, then, I thought.
I felt them lift me up and take
What seemed my body. Should I wake
And stop the darkness in my throat

And break the mist before my eyes?
I felt the bullet's leaps and swerves.
And none is loved as he deserves
And death is a disguise.

Song for a Departure

Could you indeed come lightly
Leaving no mark at all
Even of footsteps, briefly
Visit not change the air
Of this or the other room,
Have quick words with us yet be
Calm and unhurried here?

So that we should not need –
When you departed lightly
Even as swift as coming
Letting no shadow fall –
Changes, surrenders, fear,
Speeches grave to the last,
But feel no loss at all?

Lightest things in the mind
Go deep at last and can never
Be planned or weighed or lightly
Considered or set apart.
Then come like a great procession,
Touch hours with drums and flutes:
Fill all the rooms of our houses
And haunt them when you depart.

Choices

Inside the room I see the table laid,
Four chairs, a patch of light the lamp has made

And people there so deep in tenderness
They could not speak a word of happiness.

Outside I stand and see my shadow drawn
Lengthening the clipped grass of the cared-for lawn.

Above, their roof holds half the sky behind.
A dog barks bringing distances to mind.

Comfort, I think, or safety then, or both?
I warm the cold air with my steady breath.

They have designed a way to live and I,
Clothed in confusion, set their choices by:

Though sometimes one looks up and sees me there,
Alerts his shadow, pushes back his chair

And, opening windows wide, looks out at me
And close past words we stare. It seems that he

Urges my darkness, dares it to be freed
Into that room. We need each other's need.

Telling Stories

For M.

Telling you stories I forget that you
Already know the end
And I forget that I am building up
A world in which no piece must be put back
In the wrong place or time
Else you will make me go back to the start.

My scope for improvising will not ever
Deceive you into taking
A change of plan. You are so grounded in
Your absolutes, even the worlds we build
Of thin thoughts, lean ideas
You will not let us alter but expect

The thing repeated whole. Is this then what
We call your innocence –
This fine decision not to have things changed?
Is this your way of stopping clocks, of damming
The thrusting stream of time?
Has a repeated story so much power?

Such is the trust you have not in large things
But in the placing of
A verb, an adjective, a happy end.
The stories that we tell, we tell against
Ourselves then at the last
Since all the worlds we make we stand outside

Leaning on time and swayed about by it
While you stand firm within the fragile plot.

A Fear

Always to keep it in and never spare
Even a hint of pain, go guessing on,
Feigning a sacrifice, forging a tear
For someone else's grief, but still to bear
Inward the agony of self alone –

And all the masks I carry on my face,
The smile for you, the grave considered air
For you and for another some calm grace
When still within I carry an old fear
A child could never speak about, disgrace
That no confession could assuage or clear.

But once within a long and broken night
I woke and threw the shutters back for air
(The sudden moths were climbing to the light)
And from another window I saw stare
A face like mine still dream-bereft and white
And, like mine, shaken by a child's nightmare.

In a Foreign City

You cannot speak for no one knows
Your language. You must try to catch
By glances or a steadfast gaze
The attitude of those you watch.

No conversations can amaze:
Noises may find you but not speech.

Now you have circled silence, stare
With all the subtlety of sight.
Noise may trap ears but eye discerns
How someone on his elbow turns
And in the moon's long exile here
Touches another in the night.

The Roman Forum

Look at the Forum
Commanded now by Roman pines:
Walk down the ancient paths
Rubbed smooth by footprints in the past and now
Broken among the baths
And battered columns where the lizards go
In zig-zag movements like the lines
Of this decorum.

Not what the man
Who carved the column, reared the arch
Or shaped the building meant
Is what we marvel at. Perfection here
Is quite within our reach,
These ruins now are more than monument.
See how the houses disappear
Into a plan

Connived at by
Shadows of trees or light approved
By sun and not designed
By architects. Three columns eased away
From all support are moved
By how the shadows shake them from behind.
The pine trees droop their dark and sway
Swifter than eye

Can catch them all,
O and the heart is drawn to sense,
Eye and the mind are one.
The fragments here of former markets make
(Preserved by the intense
Glare of the Roman unremitting sun),
Such cities that the heart would break
And shadows fall

To see them pass.
Removed from Rome you, half-asleep,
Observe the shadows stray.
Above, the pines are playing with the light,
Dream now so dark and deep
That when you wake those columns, lucid, free,
Will burst like flowers into white
Springing from grass.

A Conversation in the Gardens of the Villa Celimontana, Rome

For A.

Deeper the shadows underneath the pines
Than their own trunks and roots. Under the hard
Blue of the sky (a Roman blue, they say)
I watched the afternoon weave its designs
Lucid as crystal on this first June day.

The fountains softly displayed themselves. The grass,
Unpressed by footprints yet, looked cool and young;
Over the paths we saw our shadows pass
And in the air the glittering moments strung
Together like a brilliance under glass.

Suddenly to this fullness our words went
Talking of visionaries, of those men
Who make a stillness deeper than an act,
Who probe beyond a place where passion's spent
And apprehend by purest intellect.

You talked of this and in between your words
I sensed (still shadowed by my own warm flesh)
That you had known such apprehensions and
Back in the garden where the pine-trees stand
Held to that moment where all hungers hush.

Yes but the garden held a stillness too.
My mind could seize upon the pleasures there,
Yet in between the fountains and the grass,
The leaning pines, the overriding air,
I glimpsed a radiance where no shadows pass.

A Roman Window

After the griefs of night,
Over the doors of day,
Here by this window-sill
I watch the climbing light
As early footsteps steal
Enormous shadows away.

Tenderly from this height
I feel compassion come –
People pestered by hours,
The morning swung to sight
As all the city stirs
And trembles in my room.

So from a stance of calm,
A stepping out of sleep,
My shadow once again
Disperses in the warm
Day with its lives more deep
Than any pleasure or pain.

Fountain

Let it disturb no more at first
Than the hint of a pool predicted far in a forest,
Or a sea so far away that you have to open
Your window to hear it.
Think of it then as elemental, as being
Necessity,
Not for a cup to be taken to it and not
For lips to linger or eye to receive itself
Back in reflection, simply
As water the patient moon persuades and stirs.

And then step closer,
Imagine rivers you might indeed embark on,
Waterfalls where you could
Silence an afternoon by staring but never
See the same tumult twice.
Yes come out of the narrow street and enter
The full piazza. Come where the noise compels.
Statues are bowing down to the breaking air.

Observe it there – the fountain, too fast for shadows,
Too wild for the lights which illuminate it to hold,
Even a moment, an ounce of water back;
Stare at such prodigality and consider
It is the elegance here, it is the taming,
The keeping fast in a thousand flowering sprays,
That builds this energy up but lets the watchers
See in that stress an image of utter calm,
A stillness there. It is how we must have felt
Once at the edge of some perpetual stream,
Fearful of touching, bringing no thirst at all,
Panicked by no perception of ourselves
But drawing the water down to the deepest wonder.

San Paolo fuori le Mura, Rome

It is the stone makes stillness here, I think
There could not be so much of silence if
The columns were not set there rank on rank,
For silence needs a shape in which to sink
And stillness needs these shadows for its life.

My darkness throws so little space before
My body where it stands, and yet my mind
Needs the large echoing churches and the roar
Of streets outside its own calm place to find
Where the soft doves of peace withdraw, withdraw.

The alabaster windows here permit
Only suggestions of the sun to slide
Into the church and make a glow in it;
The battering daylight leaps at large outside
Though what slips here through jewels seems most fit.

And here one might in his discovered calm
Feel the great building draw away from him,
His head bent closely down upon his arm,
With all the sun subsiding to a dim
Past-dreamt-of peace, a kind of coming home.

For me the senses still have their full sway
Even where prayer comes quicker than an act.
I cannot quite forget the blazing day,
The alabaster windows or the way
The light refuses to be called abstract.

Letter from Assisi

Here you will find peace, they said,
Here where silence is so wide you hear it,
Where every church you enter is a kind
Continuing of thought,
Here there is ease.
Now on this road, looking up to the hill

Where the town looks severe and seems to say
There is no softness here, no sensual joy,
Close by the flowers that fling me back to England –
The bleeding poppy and the dusty vetch
And all blue flowers reflecting back the sky –
It is not peace I feel but some nostalgia,
So that a hand which draws a shutter back,
An eye which warms as it observes a child,
Hurt me with homesickness. Peace pales and withers.

The doves demur, an English voice divides
The distances. It is the afternoon,
But here siesta has no place because
All of the day is strung with silences.
Bells wound the air and I remember one
Who long ago confided how such ringing
Brought salt into their mouth, tears to their eyes.
I think I understand a mood like that:
Doves, bells, the silent hills, O all the trappings
We dress our plans of peace in, fail me now.
I search some shadow wider than my own,
Some apprehension which requires no mood
Of local silence or a sense of prayer –
An open glance that looks from some high window
And illustrates a need I wish to share.

The Annunciation

Nothing will ease the pain to come
Though now she sits in ecstasy
And lets it have its way with her.
The angel's shadow in the room
Is lightly lifted as if he
Had never terrified her there.

The furniture again returns
To its old simple state. She can
Take comfort from the things she knows
Though in her heart new loving burns
Something she never gave to man
Or god before, and this god grows

45

Most like a man. She wonders how
To pray at all, what thanks to give
And whom to give them to. "Alone
To all men's eyes I now must go"
She thinks, "And by myself must live
With a strange child that is my own."

So from her ecstasy she moves
And turns to human things at last
(Announcing angels set aside).
It is a human child she loves
Though a god stirs beneath her breast
And great salvations grip her side.

The Visitation

She had not held her secret long enough
To covet it but wished it shared as though
Telling would tame the terrifying moment
When she, most calm in her own afternoon,
        Felt the intrepid angel, heard
His beating wings, his voice across her prayer.

This was the thing she needed to impart,
The uncalm moment, the strange interruption,
The angel bringing pain disguised as joy,
But mixed with this was something she could share
        And not abandon, simply how
A child sprang in her like the first of seeds.

And in the stillness of that other day
The afternoon exposed its emptiness,
Shadows adrift from light, the long road turning
In a dry sequence of the sun. And she
        No apprehensive figure seemed,
Only a moving silence through the land.

And all her journeying was a caressing
Within her mind of secrets to be spoken.
The simple fact of birth soon overshadowed

46

The shadow of the angel. When she came
    Close to her cousin's house she kept
Only the message of her happiness.

And those two women in their quick embrace
Gazed at each other with looks undisturbed
By men or miracles. It was the child
Who laid his shadow on their afternoon
    By stirring suddenly, by bringing
Back the broad echoes of those beating wings.

Teresa of Avila

Spain. The wild dust, the whipped corn, earth easy for footsteps,
shallow to starving seeds. High sky at night like walls. Silences
surrounding Avila.

She, teased by questions, aching for reassurance. Calm in
confession before incredulous priests. Then back – to the pure
illumination, the profound personal prayer, the four waters.

Water from the well first, drawn up painfully. Clinking of pails.
Dry lips at the well-head. Parched grass bending. And the dry
heart too – waiting for prayer.

Then the water-wheel, turning smoothly. Somebody helping
unseen. A keen hand put out, gently sliding the wheel. Then
water and the aghast spirit refreshed and quenched.

Not this only. Other waters also, clear from a spring or a pool.
Pouring from a fountain like child's play – but the child is else-
where. And she, kneeling, cooling her spirit at the water, comes
nearer, nearer.

Then the entire cleansing, utterly from nowhere. No wind ruffled
it, no shadows slid across it. Her mind met it, her will approved.
And all beyonds, backwaters, dry words of old prayers were lost
in it. The water was only itself.

And she knelt there, waited for the shadows to cross the light which the water made, waited for familiar childhood illuminations (the lamp by the bed, the candle in church, sun beckoned by horizons) – but this light was none of these, was only how the water looked, how the will turned and was still. Even the image of light itself withdrew, and the dry dust on the winds of Spain outside her halted. Moments spread not into hours but stood still. No dove brought the tokens of peace. She was the peace that her prayers had promised. And the silences suffered no shadows.

Song for a Birth or a Death

Last night I saw the savage world
And heard the blood beat up the stair;
The fox's bark, the owl's shrewd pounce,
The crying creatures – all were there,
And men in bed with love and fear.

The slit moon only emphasised
How blood must flow and teeth must grip.
What does the calm light understand,
The light which draws the tide and ship
And drags the owl upon its prey
And human creatures lip to lip?

Last night I watched how pleasure must
Leap from disaster with its will:
The fox's fear, the watch-dog's lust
Know that all matings mean a kill:
And human creatures kissed in trust
Feel the blood throb to death until

The seed is struck, the pleasure's done,
The birds are thronging in the air;
The moon gives way to widespread sun.
Yes but the pain still crouches where
The young fox and the child are trapped
And cries of love are cries of fear.

Family Affairs

No longer here the blaze that we'd engender
Out of pure wrath. We pick at quarrels now
As fussy women stitch at cotton, slow
Now to forget and too far to surrender.
The anger stops, apologies also.

And in this end of summer, weighted calm
(Climate of mind, I mean), we are apart
Further than ever when we wished most harm.
Indifference lays a cold hand on the heart;
We need the violence to keep us warm.

Have we then learnt at last how to untie
The bond of birth, umbilical long cord,
So that we live quite unconnected by
The blood we share? What monstrous kind of sword
Can sever veins and still we do not die?

A Game of Chess

The quiet moves, the gently shaded room:
It is like childhood once again when I
Sat with a tray of toys and you would come
To take my temperature and make me lie
Under the clothes and sleep. Now peacefully

We sit above the intellectual game.
Pure mathematics seems to rule the board
Emotionless. And yet I feel the same
As when I sat and played without a word
Inventing kingdoms where great feelings stirred.

Is it that knight and king and small squat castle
Store up emotion, bring it under rule,
So that the problems now with which we wrestle
Seem simply of the mind? Do feelings cool
Beneath the order of an abstract school?

Never entirely, since the whole thing brings
Me back to childhood when I was distressed:
You seem the same who put away my things
At night, my toys and tools of childish lust.
My king is caught now in a world of trust.

My Grandmother

She kept an antique shop – or it kept her.
Among Apostle spoons and Bristol glass,
The faded silks, the heavy furniture,
She watched her own reflection in the brass
Salvers and silver bowls, as if to prove
Polish was all, there was no need of love.

And I remember how I once refused
To go out with her, since I was afraid.
It was perhaps a wish not to be used
Like antique objects. Though she never said
That she was hurt, I still could feel the guilt
Of that refusal, guessing how she felt.

Later, too frail to keep a shop, she put
All her best things in one long narrow room.
The place smelt old, of things too long kept shut,
The smell of absences where shadows come
That can't be polished. There was nothing then
To give her own reflection back again.

And when she died I felt no grief at all,
Only the guilt of what I once refused.
I walked into her room among the tall
Sideboards and cupboards – things she never used
But needed; and no finger-marks were there,
Only the new dust falling through the air.

In Praise of Creation

That one bird, one star,
The one flash of the tiger's eye
Purely assert what they are,
Without ceremony testify.

Testify to order, to rule –
How the birds mate at one time only,
How the sky is, for a certain time, full
Of birds, the moon sometimes cut thinly.

And the tiger trapped in the cage of his skin,
Watchful over creation, rests
For the blood to pound, the drums to begin,
Till the tigress' shadow casts

A darkness over him, a passion, a scent,
The world goes turning, turning, the season
Sieves earth to its one sure element
And the blood beats beyond reason.

Then quiet, and birds folding their wings,
The new moon waiting for years to be stared at here,
The season sinks to satisfied things –
Man with his mind ajar.

World I Have Not Made

I have sometimes thought how it would have been
if I had had to create the whole thing myself –
my life certainly but also something else;
I mean a world which I could inhabit freely,
ideas, objects, everything prepared;
not ideas simply as Plato knew them,
shadows of shadows, but more like furniture,
something to move around and live in,
something I had made. But still there would be
all that I hadn't made – animals, stars,
tides tugging against me, moon uncaring,

and the trying to love without reciprocity.
All this is here still. It is hard, hard,
even with free faith outlooking boundaries,
to come to terms with obvious suffering.
I live in a world I have not created
inward or outward. There is a sweetness
in willing surrender: I trail my ideas
behind great truths. My ideas are like shadows
and sometimes I consider how it would have been
to create a credo, objects, ideas
and then to live with them. I can understand
when tides most tug and the moon is remote
and the trapped wild beast is one with its shadow,
how even great faith leaves room for abysses
and the taut mind turns to its own requirings.

Harvest and Consecration

After the heaped piles and the cornsheaves waiting
To be collected, gathered into barns,
After all fruits have burst their skins, the sating
    Season cools and turns,
And then I think of something that you said
Of when you held the chalice and the bread.

I spoke of Mass and thought of it as close
To how a season feels which stirs and brings
Fire to the hearth, food to the hungry house
    And strange, uncovered things –
God in a garden then in sheaves of corn
And the white bread a way to be reborn.

I thought of priest as midwife and as mother
Feeling the pain, feeling the pleasure too,
    All opposites together,
Until you said no one could feel such passion
And still preserve the power of consecration.

And it is true. How cool the gold sheaves lie,
Rich without need to ask for any more
Richness. The seed, the simple thing must die
    If only to restore
Our faith in fruitful, hidden things. I see
The wine and bread protect our ecstasy.

A World of Light

Yes when the dark withdrew I suffered light
And saw the candles heave beneath the wax,
I watched the shadows of my old self dwindle
As softly on my recollection stole
A mood the senses could not touch or damage,
A sense of peace beyond the breathing word.

Day dawdled at my elbow. It was night
Within. I saw my hands, their soft dark backs
Keeping me from the noise outside. The candle
Seemed snuffed into a deep and silent pool:
It drew no shadow round my constant image
For in a dazzling dark my spirit stirred.

But still I questioned it. My inward sight
Still knew the senses and the senses' tracks,
I felt my flesh and clothes, a rubbing sandal,
And distant voices wishing to console.
My mind was keen to understand and rummage
To find assurance in the sounds I heard.

Then senses ceased and thoughts were driven quite
Away (no act of mine). I could relax
And feel a fire no earnest prayer can kindle;
Old parts of peace dissolved into a whole
And like a bright thing proud in its new plumage
My mind was keen as an attentive bird.

Yes, fire, light, air, birds, wax, the sun's own height
I draw from now, but every image breaks.
Only a child's simplicity can handle

Such moments when the hottest fire feels cool,
And every breath is like a sudden homage
To peace that penetrates and is not feared.

Notes for a Book of Hours

I

Kneeling to pray and resting on the words
I feel a stillness that I have not made.
Shadows take root, the falling light is laid
Smoothly on stone and skin. I lean towards
Some meaning that's delayed.

It is as if the mind had nervous fingers,
Could touch and apprehend yet not possess.
The light is buried where the darkness lingers
And something grateful in me wants to bless
Simply from happiness.

The world dreams through me in this sudden spring.
My senses itch although the stillness stays.
God is too large a word for me to sing,
Some touch upon my spirit strums and plays:
What images will bring

This moment down to words that I can use
When not so rapt? The hours, the hours increase.
All is a movement, shadows now confuse,
Darkening the soft wings of the doves of peace,
And can I tame or choose?

II

I have to start the whole thing from the source,
Go back behind the noisy tower of tongues,
Press on my words new meanings, make my songs
Like breath from uncontaminated lungs
Or water from a new-found water-course.

Not to convince you, that it is not my aim,
Simply to speak and to be gladly heard.
I have the oils, the waters, but the name
Eludes me still. Within a single word
I want the christening, the flowering flame.

Men had it once who carved far out of sight
Demons and angels, all anonymous;
Skill was another name for pure delight.
My angels must convince, be obvious.
I must create the substance and the light.

The cosmic vision fades. Within my mind
The images are laid, books on a shelf
Dusty and old. I only need to find
Some way to show the struggle in myself –
The demons watchful but the angels blind.

III

In the cool cloisters and the choirs I hear
The open-handed words, the pleading psalms.
The chant is sober and it soothes and calms
Though what the words depict is full of fear;
I gather all the shadows in my arms.

I cannot sing but only hear and trace
The meaning underneath the echoes, wait
For the resumption of a scattered state.
Such concentration screwed into my face –
Can it reflect an inner mood of grace?

What do they think who kneel within those stalls,
Young, old, white, black? The world outside still gropes
Not for a paradise but for its hopes
Come true in time. The chanting sinks and falls –
The great bell silent, none to pull the ropes.

IV

The sound is ordered, cool.
I heard somebody say
Once that the liturgy is diffused

Theology. I think they meant the way
The music and the words are used,
Austere yet beautiful.

A world of dogma can
Within these hours be pressed.
Both day and night are counted by
The times of exhortation and of rest.
The psalms can both rejoice and sigh,
Serve every need of man.

I need to make my own
Great books of hours, record
Matins and lauds, prime, terce and vespers,
With no authority but my own word.
The psalms are loud with truth; in whispers
I mark my hours alone.

A Requiem

It is the ritual not the fact
That brings a held emotion to
Its breaking-point. This man I knew
Only a little, by his death
Shows me a love I thought I lacked
And all the stirrings underneath.

It is the calm, the solemn thing,
Not the distracted mourner's cry
Or the cold place where dead things lie,
That teaches me I cannot claim
To stand aside. These tears which sting –
Are they from sorrow or from shame?

John of the Cross

Emptiness, space. Darkness you could put walls round, set stars
in, light from far off but never thinkingly enter. To approach was
to become the darkness, not even assisted by shadows.

And the senses, too, disarmed, discouraged, withdrawn by choice from pleasure. Fingers not touching, crushing cool leaves. Lips closed against mouth or assuagement. Ears unentered by voices. Hands held out but empty. Even the darkness could not be possessed.

All indescribable then, but still the urge to depict, descry, point out, picture, prepare. The deep darkness had to be spoken of, touched beyond reach of stars, entered without indications.

Flame, then, firm – not the inward flame of passion, urgent, wanting appeasement, close to the senses and sighing through them: but a pure light pouring through windows, flooding the glass but leaving the glass unaltered.

More than this too. Not light limited by tapers, drawn to its strength by the darkness around it, not puffed out by wind or increased by careful breath.

It is held in being by patience, by watching, suffering beyond signs or words. Not your light either. You are receiver, requirer. And when the flame falters nothing of yours can revive it: you are resigned to the darkness. And you open your eyes to the world.

The Resurrection

I was the one who waited in the garden
Doubting the morning and the early light.
I watched the mist lift off its own soft burden,
Permitting not believing my own sight.

If there were sudden noises I dismissed
Them as a trick of sound, a sleight of hand.
Not by a natural joy could I be blessed
Or trust a thing I could not understand.

Maybe I was a shadow thrown by some
Who, weeping, came to lift away the stone,
Or was I but the path on which the sun,
Too heavy for itself, was loosed and thrown?

I heard the voices and the recognition
And love like kisses heard behind the walls.
Were they my tears which fell, a real contrition?
Or simply April with its waterfalls?

It was by negatives I learnt my place.
The garden went on growing and I sensed
A sudden breeze that blew across my face.
Despair returned but now it danced, it danced.

Mantegna's Agony in the Garden

The agony is formal; three
Bodies are stretched in pure repose,
One's halo leans against a tree,
Over a book his fingers close:
One's arms are folded carefully.

The third man lies with sandalled feet
Thrust in the path. They almost touch
Three playful rabbits. Down the street,
Judas and his procession march
Making the distance seem discreet.

Even the praying figure has
A cared-for attitude. This art
Puts down the city and the mass
Of mountains like a counterpart
Of pain disguised as gentleness.

And yet such careful placing here
Of mountain, men and agony,
Being so solid makes more clear
The pain. Pain is particular.
The foreground shows a barren tree:
Is it a vulture crouching there,
No symbol but a prophecy?

Visit to an Artist

For David Jones

Window upon the wall, a balcony
With a light chair, the air and water so
Mingled you could not say which was the sun
And which the adamant yet tranquil spray.
But nothing was confused and nothing slow:
Each way you looked, always the sea, the sea.

And every shyness that we brought with us
Was drawn into the pictures on the walls.
It was so good to sit quite still and lose
Necessity of discourse, words to choose
And wonder which were honest and which false.

Then I remembered words that you had said
Of art as gesture and as sacrament,
A mountain under the calm form of paint
Much like the Presence under wine and bread –
Art with its largesse and its own restraint.

The Clown

I

Balloon on finger he watches us, the clown;
White cheeks conceal what eyes are witness of
And nimble body hides in pantaloon.
If you love this it is yourself you love,
Your own absurdity, your pride brought down.

But is this what he means, or does he mean
A dancing childish world where play is fact?
The rubber ball returns unburst and clean –
Your world so shapely, blown up but intact?
Are you the dancer in a pasteboard scene?

I am afraid of things which can be hurt.
The clown as much as cringing animals
Invites my wounding. Yet my pain will start

59

Because I wound. The clown prevails in art;
Gently as his balloon, my pity falls.

II

Aloof, reserved, yet strangely vulnerable,
Making of art a nonchalance, mere skill

As though a skill were something not to care
Too much about. You throw balls in the air,

You make yourself ridiculous, your face
Fitting nowhere but in a taut white space.

Yet sometimes carelessly you have been drawn
By painters in their note-book moments when

A special care appears but fits nowhere –
A harlequin who leans upon a chair,

A youth who idly strums an old guitar,
Each lazy gesture meaning "I don't care."

III

Others are noble and admired –
The ones who walk the tightrope without nets,
The one who goes inside the lion's cage,
And all the grave, audacious acrobats.
Away from fear and rage
He simply is the interval for tired

People who cannot bear
Too much excitement. They can see in him
Their own lost innocence or else their fear
(For him no metal bars or broken limb).
Have they forgotten that it takes as much
Boldness to tumble, entertain and jest
When loneliness walks tightropes in your breast
And every joke is like a wild beast's touch?

IV

If I painted you
It would not be as juggler or as one who
Played the fool and entertained the crowds.
I would have you entirely alone,
Thoughtful and leaning
Against a dark window that needed cleaning.

I would want to show you
Not as victim or scapegoat,
Not like one who is hurried away, loaded
With other people's fears, goaded
Into the distance, but rather
As one who uses distance as a tether,
Tied but detached,
Sympathetic yet remote.

Strangely you remind
Of Christ on the cross.
Is it the seeming surrender or the white face,
The acceptance of loss?
Or simply that you seem like one not fallen from grace,
Innocent through knowledge,
Assenting yet resigned?

V

The eager one unconscious of himself,
Drawing the the bow across the strings, absorbed
In music or the version that he makes,

The smiling one who never seems afraid,
Something to offer always yet not hoarding
His own or others' thoughts of what he is –

Simply the one who does not analyse
But still can gauge the feelings that surround him,
Loosen the taut voice, spread the narrow smile.

My childhood stands abruptly at my elbow
Forbidding demonstration, looking in,
Seeing the wishes and the dancers there.

Something he has to say
Concerning pain. You have to watch the dance
With utmost concentration, in the way
A child will watch until the view enchants
And he is lost in it. The clown is gay
    And terrible at once.

His face will never show
You any hint of what you ought to feel:
White greasepaint spreads across his cheeks like snow.
His jokes seem feeble and his tricks are slow,
    He seems a game, unreal.

And yet his helplessness,
His lack of tragic gesture, tragic mood,
Remind me of the abject beast we press
Our own despairs on, Christ nailed to the wood.
There are more ways to make a wilderness
    Than we have understood.

Lazarus

It was the amazing white, it was the way he simply
Refused to answer our questions, it was the cold pale glance
Of death upon him, the smell of death that truly
Declared his rising to us. It was no chance
Happening, as a man may fill a silence
Between two heart-beats, seem to be dead and then
Astonish us with the closeness of his presence;
This man was dead, I say it again and again.
All of our sweating bodies moved towards him
And our minds moved too, hungry for finished faith.
He would not enter our world at once with words
That we might be tempted to twist or argue with:
Cold like a white root pressed in the bowels of earth
He looked, but also vulnerable – like birth.

The Diamond Cutter

Not what the light will do but how he shapes it
And what particular colours it will bear,

And something of the climber's concentration
Seeing the white peak, setting the right foot there.

Not how the sun was plausible at morning
Nor how it was distributed at noon,

And not how much the single stone could show
But rather how much brilliance it would shun;

Simply a paring down, a cleaving to
One object, as the star-gazer who sees

One single comet polished by its fall
Rather than countless, untouched galaxies.

Stargazers and Others

One, staring out stars,
Lost himself in looking and almost
Forgot glass, eye, air, space;
Simply, he thought, the world is improved
By my staring, how the still glass leaps
When the sky thuds in like tides.

Another, making love, once
Stared so far over his pleasure
That woman, world, the spiral
Of taut bodies, the clinging hands, broke apart
And he saw, as the stargazer sees,
Landscapes made to be looked at,
Fruit to fall, not be plucked.

In you also something
Of such vision occurs.
How else would I have learnt
The tapered stars, the pause

On the nervous spiral? Names I need
Stronger than love, desire,
Passion, pleasure. O discover
Some star and christen it, but let me be
The space that your eye moves over.

To a Friend with a Religious Vocation

For C.

Thinking of your vocation, I am filled
With thoughts of my own lack of one. I see
Within myself no wish to breed or build
Or take the three vows ringed by poverty.
    And yet I have a sense,
Vague and inchoate, with no symmetry,
Of purpose. Is it merely a pretence,

A kind of scaffolding which I erect
Half out of fear, half out of laziness?
The fitful poems come but can't protect
The empty areas of loneliness
    You know what you must do,
So that mere breathing is a way to bless.
Dark nights, perhaps, but no grey days for you.

Your vows enfold you. I must make my own;
Now this, now that, each one empirical.
My poems move from feelings not yet known,
And when a poem is written I can feel
    A flash, a moment's peace.
The curtain will be drawn across your grille.
My silences are always enemies.

Yet with the same convictions that you have
(It is but your vocation that I lack),
I must, like you, believe in perfect love.
It is the dark, the dark that draws me back
    Into a chaos where
Vocations, visions fail, the will grows slack
And I am stunned by silence everywhere.

Greek Statues

These I have never touched but only looked at.
If you could say that stillness means surrender
These are surrendered,
Yet their large audacious gestures signify surely
Remonstrance, reprisal? What have they left to lose
But the crumbling away by rain or time? Defiance
For them is a dignity, a declaration.

Odd how one wants to touch not simply stare,
To run one's finger over the flanks and arms,
Not to possess, rather to be possessed.
Bronze is bright to the eye but under the hands
Is cool and calming. Gods into silent metal:

To stone also, not to the palpable flesh.
Incarnations are elsewhere and more human,
Something concerning us; but these are other.
It is as if something infinite, remote
Permitted intrusion. It is as if these blind eyes
Exposed a landscape precious with grapes and olives:
And our probing hands move not to grasp but praise.

The Pride of Life: A Roman Setting

Old men discourse upon wise topics here:
Children and women pass the shadows by,
Only the young are desperate. Their clear
And unambiguous gazes strike
Against each brushing hand or eye,
Their faces like

O something far away, maybe a cave
Where looks and actions always moved to hunt,
Where every gesture knew how to behave
And there was never space between
The easy having and the want.
I think the keen

Primitive stares that pierce this decorous street
Look in some far back mood and time to claim
A life beyond the urbane and effete
Where youth from coolest childhood came,
    And look to look was like the hunter's throw –
    Perpetually new and long ago.

Men Fishing in the Arno

I do not know what they are catching,
I only know that they stand there, leaning
A little like lovers, eager but not demanding,
Waiting and hoping for a catch, money,
A meal tomorrow but today, still there, steady.

And the river also moves as calmly
From the waterfall slipping to a place
A mind could match its thought with.
And above, the cypresses with cool gestures
Command the city, give it formality.

It is like this every day but more especially
On Sundays: every few yards you see a fisherman,
Each independent, none
Working with others and yet accepting
Others. From this one might, I think,

Build a whole way of living – men in their mazes
Of secret desires yet keeping a sense
Of order outwardly, hoping
Not too flamboyantly, satisfied with little
Yet not surprised should the river suddenly
Yield a hundredfold, every hunger appeased.

Two Deaths

It was only a film,
Perhaps I shall say later
Forgetting the story, left only

With bright images – the blazing dawn
Over the European ravaged plain,
And a white unsaddled horse, the only calm
Living creature. Will only such pictures remain?

Or shall I see
The shot boy running, running
Clutching the white sheet on the washing-line,
Looking at his own blood like a child
Who never saw blood before and feels defiled,
A boy dying without dignity
Yet brave still, trying to stop himself from falling
And screaming – his white girl waiting just out of calling?

I am ashamed
Not to have seen anyone dead,
Anyone I know I mean;
Odd that yesterday also
I saw a broken cat stretched on a path,
Not quite finished. Its gentle head
Showed one eye staring, mutely beseeching
Death, it seemed. All day
I have thought of death, of violence and death,
Of the blazing Polish light, of the cat's eye:
I am ashamed I have never seen anyone die.

About These Things

About these things I always shall be dumb.
Some wear their silences as more than dress,
As more than skin-deep. I bear mine like some

Scar that is hidden out of shamefulness.
I speak from depths I do not understand
Yet cannot find the words for this distress.

So much of power is put into my hand
When words come easily. I sense the way
People are charmed and pause; I seem to mend

Some hurt. Some healing seems to make them stay.
And yet within the power that I use
My wordless fears remain. Perhaps I say

In lucid verse the terrors that confuse
In conversation. Maybe I am dumb
Because if fears were spoken I would lose

The lovely languages I do not choose
More than the darknesses from which they come.

The Unfulfilled

It was love only that we knew
At first. We did not dispossess
Each other of the total view
That is quite blurred when passions pass.
I felt myself, acknowledged you.

When did desire enter and
Confuse the sweetness, heat the blood?
On meeting we could understand,
Wordless, each other's every mood.
Where does love start and friendship end?

Impediments have set apart
The impulse from fruition. We,
Who have no compass but the heart,
Must learn an immaturity,
Though all the later passions hurt.

By acts of will we now must find
Each other as we were at first,
Unthwarted then and unconfined.
Yes, but I have an aching thirst
That can't be quenched by a cool mind.

We must stand side by side and live
As if the past were still to come.
It is our needs we need to give

And fashion from their anguish some
Love that has no wish to deceive
But rests contented, being dumb.

The Instruments

Only in our imaginations
The act is done, for you have spoken
Vows that can never now be broken.
I keep them too – with reservations;
Yet acts not done can still be taken
Away, like all completed passions.

But what can not be taken is
Satiety. Cool space lies near
Our bodies – a parenthesis
Between a pleasure and a fear.
Our loving is composed of this
Touching of strings to make sounds clear.

A touching, then a glancing off.
It is your vows that stretch between
Us like an instrument of love
Where only echoes intervene.
Yet these exchanges are enough
Since strings touched only are most keen.

Remembering Fireworks

Always as if for the first time we watch
The fireworks as if no one had ever
Done this before, made shapes, signs,
Cut diamonds on air, sent up stars
Nameless, imperious. And in the falling
Of fire, the spent rocket, there is a kind
Of nostalgia as normally only attaches
To things long known and lost. Such an absence,

69

Such emptiness of sky the fireworks leave
After their festival. We, fumbling
For words of love, remember the rockets,
The spinning wheels, the sudden diamonds,
And say with delight "Yes, like that, like that."
Oh and the air is full of falling
Stars surrendered. We search for a sign.

from Michelangelo's Sonnets

II   On Dante Alighieri

It is not possible to say how much
We owe to him, because his splendour blinds
Our eyes. Simpler it is to blame those minds
Too small to honour him, to sense his touch.

He did not fear to plumb to places where
Failure alone survives. But this was done
For our example. Always he was near
To God. Only his country dared to shun

His greatness. Her ingratitude at last
Turned on herself. As proof of this, observe
How always to the perfect sorrows fall

Most painfully. To those who are the best
Most ill occurs. Dante did not deserve
Exile; his equal never lived at all.

III   To Pope Julius II

My Lord, of all the ancient proverbs, this
Is surely true – "Who *can* doth never will".
You have believed in saws and promises
And blest those men whom falsehoods, not truths, fill.

Always I have been faithful and would give
Honour to you as rays do to the sun.
Yet all my pain has never made you grieve,
The less I please, the more work I have done.

70

Once I had hoped to climb by means of your
Great height, but now I find we rather need
Justice and power, not echoes faint indeed.

Heaven, it appears, itself is made impure
When worldliness has power. I live to take
Fruit from a tree too dry to bear or break.

VII   *To Luigi del Riccio*

It happens sometimes even in the great
Sweetness of courtesy, of life and honour,
That an offence can hide. Thus, in this manner
Some good is spoilt and mars my healthy state.

He who can give to others wings of hope
Yet stretch a hidden net along their way,
Is false to the great fire of charity
And brings true friendship to a sudden stop.

Therefore, keep clear, Luigi, that first grace
To which I owe my life, let no storm mar
Its calm, let no wind stir its steady peace.

Contempt can make all gratitude obscure,
But, with true friendship, nothing can displace
Its strength. For this, pain is a way to please.

X   *To Gandolfo Porrino on his Mistress Faustina Mancina*

Unique in heaven as on this wicked earth
(Though cheaply by the vulgar crowd is she
Named – that crowd, too blind to see her worth),
The new high beauty was designed to be

For you alone. Neither with tools nor pen
Would I know how to fashion her or trace
The radiant beauty of her living face.
For that, you must return to life again.

And if she overwhelms imagination
As the great sun outshines the other stars,
Still you may rate her at her real price.

71

To calm your pining and your desolation
God moulds her beauty which can far surpass
All I can make. My art will not suffice.

XIII

To be more worthy of you, Lady, is
My sole desire. For all your kindnesses
I try to show, with all I have of art,
And courtesy, the gladness of my heart.

But well I know that simply by my own
Efforts I cannot match your goodness. Then
I ask you pardon for what's left undone,
And failing thus, I grow more wise again.

Indeed, I know it would be wrong to hope
That favours, raining from you as from heaven,
Could be repaid by human work so frail.

Art, talent, memory, with all their scope
Can never pay you back what you have given.
At this, a thousand tries would always fail.

XVI

Just as in pen and ink, the high and low
And mediocre styles can find expression,
And as in marbles the imagination,
Noble or base, will its own worth bestow;

So, my dear Lord, whatever finds its place
Within your heart – pride or humility –
I draw from it only what moves in me,
As you can tell from what shows on my face.

For he who sows both sighs and tears will find
(Since heaven, whose dew is always pure and clear,
To different seeds will variously appear),

That what he reaps is sorrow. Heart and mind,
When grievously afflicted, still will see
In greatest beauty only misery.

Lady, how can it be that what is shown
Through long experience and imagination
Endures so long in hard and mountain stone,
While years enact the maker's consummation?

The cause to the effect yields and gives place,
Nature by art is overcome at last.
I know too well who work with sculptor's grace
That time and death resign me to the past.

Thus can I give long life to you and me
In one way, either in stone or else in paint
Which seems to show each other's faces true.

Thus, in a thousand years all men shall see
How beautiful you were, how I was faint
And yet how wise I was in loving you.

XX

How much a garland pleases when it lies,
Woven with flowers, upon some golden hair;
It seems as if each blossom thrusts and tries
To be the first to kiss that forehead fair.

Contented all day long that garment is
Which spreads itself but first clings to her breast.
The golden threat asks nothing but to rest,
Touching her cheeks and throat with tenderness.

More honoured still that ribbon which can lie,
Gilded and shaped in the most cunning fashion,
Touching the breast which it so carefully laces.

And that small belt that knots so easily
Seems to declare, "Unceasing my caresses."
Would that my arms might join in such a passion!

XXXIV   To Tommaso de Cavalieri

Eternal fire is kindly to cold stone
And draws strength from it. And though stone may fall
To ashes, it has never really gone
But lives in fire and is not lost at all.

And if, in furnaces, through every season
It lasts, it has achieved a higher place,
Just as a purged soul moves from its own prison
And flies to heaven adorned with every grace.

It is the same with me when fierce desires
Reduce me to pale ashes, dry and cold:
I am not lost but find new life indeed.

If I can rise from ashes which seem dead
And come unscathed from these consuming fires,
I am not forged from iron but from gold.

LV

My Lord, you know that I know that you know
That I have come to be more close, more near.
You know that I know what is known to you,
Why then do we delay in greeting here?

If all that you have said is really true,
And if, which you admit, my trust is real,
Then break the wall dividing us, and know
A double strength can greater woes conceal.

If in you, I love only, my dear Lord,
What you love more yourself, do not be hurt
That with one soul another should accord.

That in your noble face which I love most
Is scarcely known by human mind and heart.
He who would see it must become a ghost.

LXVII   *To Giorgio Vasari*

There is no lower thing on earth than I
Conceive myself to be when I lack you.
My weak and tired spirit makes me sigh
For pardon for all things I've failed to do.

Stretch down to me, Oh God, that powerful chain
That knots all heavenly gifts. Such faith and trust
Are what I long forever to attain;
It is my fault I am not fully blest.

The more I think of faith, more rare and good
It seems, and even greater may it be
Since all the world depends on it for peace.

You never were a miser of your blood:
If Heaven is locked to every other key,
What kind of gifts of mercy, then, are these?

LXXI

Now that I need men's pity and compassion,
And can no longer scoff and laugh at all
The faults of others, now my soul must fall
Unguided, lacking its own domination.

Only one flag can I now serve beneath,
And with it conquer life. I speak of faith.
Only with this can I face the attack
Of all my foes, when other help I lack.

Oh flesh, Oh blood, Oh wood, Oh pain extreme!
Let all my sins be purified through you
From whom I came, as did my father too.

So good you are, your pity is supreme;
Only your help can save my evil fate:
So close to death, so far from God my state.

LXXV

I wish, God, for some end I do not will.
Between the fire and heart a veil of ice
Puts out the fire. My pen will not move well,
So that the sheet on which I'm working lies.

I pay you mere lip-service, then I grieve;
Love does not reach my heart, I do not know
How to admit that grace which would relieve
My state and crush the arrogance I show.

Oh tear away that veil, God, break that wall
Which with its strength refuses to let in
The sun whose light has vanished from the world.

Send down the promised light to bless and hold
Your lovely bride. So may I seek for all
I need in you, both end there and begin.

LXXVII

Although it saddens me and causes pain,
The past, which is not with me any more,
Brings me relief, since all that I abhor –
My sin and guilt – will not come back again.

Precious it is to me because I learn,
Before death comes, how brief is happiness:
But sad also, since when at last I turn
For pardon, grace may yet refuse to bless.

Although, Oh God, your promise I attend,
It is too much to ask you to forgive
Those who for pardon have so long delayed.

But in the blood you shed, I understand
What recompense and mercy you've displayed,
Showering your precious gifts that we may live.

LXXVIII

Dear to me is sleep: still more, being made of stone.
While pain and guilt still linger here below,
Blindness and numbness – these please me alone;
Then do not wake me, keep your voices low.

Sequence in Hospital

I *Pain*

At my wits' end
And all resources gone, I lie here,
All of my body tense to the touch of fear,
And my mind,

Muffled now as if the nerves
Refused any longer to let thoughts form,
Is no longer a safe retreat, a tidy home,
No longer serves

My body's demands or shields
With fine words, as it once would daily,
My storehouse of dread. Now, slowly,
My heart, hand, whole body yield

To fear. Bed, ward, window begin
To lose their solidity. Faces no longer
Look kind or needed; yet I still fight the stronger
Terror – oblivion – the needle thrusts in.

II   *The Ward*

One with the photographs of grandchildren,
Another with discussion of disease,

Another with the memory of her garden,
Another with her marriage – all of these

Keep death at bay by building round their illness
A past they never honoured at the time.

The sun streams through the window, the earth heaves
Gently for this new season. Blossoms climb

Out on the healthy world where no one thinks
Of pain. Nor would these patients wish them to;

The great preservers here are little things –
The dream last night, a photograph, a view.

III   *After an Operation*

What to say first? I learnt I was afraid,
Not frightened in the way that I had been
When wide awake and well, I simply mean
Fear became absolute and I became
Subject to it; it beckoned, I obeyed.

Fear which before had been particular,
Attached to this or that scene, word, event,
Here became general. Past, future meant
Nothing. Only the present moment bore
This huge, vague fear, this wish for nothing more.

Yet life still stirred and nerves themselves became
Like shoots which hurt while growing, sensitive
To find not death but further ways to live.
And now I'm convalescent, fear can claim
No general power. Yet I am not the same.

IV *Patients in a Public Ward*

Like children now, bed close to bed,
With flowers set up where toys would be
In real childhoods, secretly
We cherish each our own disease,
And when we talk we talk to please
Ourselves that still we are not dead.

All is kept safe – the healthy world
Held at a distance, on a rope.
Where human things like hate and hope
Persist. The world we know is full
Of things we need, unbeautiful
And yet desired – a glass to hold

And sip, a cube of ice, a pill
To help us sleep. Yet in this warm
And sealed-off nest, the least alarm
Speaks clear of death. Our fears grow wide;
There are no places left to hide
And no more peace in lying still.

V *The Visitors*

They visit me and I attempt to keep
A social smile upon my face. Even here
Some ceremony is required, no deep
Relationship, simply a way to clear
    Emotion to one side; the fear
I felt last night is buried in drugged sleep.

They come and all their kindness makes me want
To cry (they say the sick weep easily).
When they have gone I shall be limp and faint,
My heart will thump and stumble crazily;
     Yet through my illness I can see
One wish stand clear no pain, no fear can taint.

Your absence has been stronger than all pain
And I am glad to find that when most weak
Always my mind returned to you again.
Through all the noisy nights when, harsh awake,
     I longed for day and light to break –
In that sick desert, you were life, were rain.

VI *Hospital*

Observe the hours which seem to stand
Between these beds and pause until
A shriek breaks through the time to show
That humankind is suffering still.

Observe the tall and shrivelled flowers,
So brave a moment to the glance.
The fevered eyes stare through the hours
And petals fall with soft foot-prints.

A world where silence has no hold
Except a tentative small grip.
Limp hands upon the blankets fold,
Minds from their bodies slowly slip.

Though death is never talked of here,
It is more palpable and felt –
Touching the cheek or in a tear –
By being present by default.

The muffled cries, the curtains drawn,
The flowers pale before they fall –
The world itself is here brought down
To what is suffering and small.

The huge philosophies depart,
Large words slink off, like faith, like love,

The thumping of the human heart
Is reassurance here enough.

Only one dreamer going back
To how he felt when he was well,
Weeps under pillows at his lack
But cannot tell, but cannot tell.

VII   *For a Woman with a Fatal Illness*

The verdict has been given and you lie quietly
Beyond hope, hate, revenge, even self-pity.

You accept gratefully the gifts – flowers, fruit –
Clumsily offered now that your visitors too

Know you must certainly die in a matter of months,
They are dumb now, reduced only to gestures,

Helpless before your news, perhaps hating
You because you are the cause of their unease.

I, too, watching from my temporary corner,
Feel impotent and wish for something violent –

Whether as sympathy only, I am not sure –
But something at least to break the terrible tension.

Death has no right to come so quietly.

VIII   *Patients*

Violence does not terrify.
Storms here would be a relief,
Lightning be a companion to grief.
It is the helplessness, the way they lie

Beyond hope, fear, love,
That makes me afraid. I would like to shout,
Crash my voice into the silence, flout
The passive suffering here. They move

Only in pain, their bodies no longer seem
Dependent on blood, muscle, bone.
It is as if air alone
Kept them alive, or else a mere whim

On the part of instrument, surgeon, nurse.
I too am one of them, but well enough
To long for some simple sign of life,
Or to imagine myself getting worse.

Works of Art

So often it appears like an escape,
That cool, wide world where even shadows are
Ordered and relegated to a shape
Not too intrusive and yet not too spare.
How easy it has seemed to wander deep
Into this world and find a shelter there.

Yet always it surprises. Nervous hands
Which make the first rough sketch in any art,
Leave their own tension, and the statue stands,
The poem lies with trouble at its heart.
And every fashioned object makes demands
Though we feel uncommitted at the start.

Yeats said that gaiety explained it all,
That Hamlet, Lear were gay, and so are we.
He did not look back to a happy Fall
Where man stood lost, ashamed beneath a tree.
There was no art within that garden wall
Until we chose our dangerous liberty.

And now all making has the bitter-sweet
Taste of frustration yet of something done.
We want more order than we ever meet
And art keeps driving us most hopefully on.
Yet coolness is derived from all that heat,
And shadows draw attention to the sun.

Man in a Park

One lost in thought of what his life might mean
Sat in a park and watched the children play,
Did nothing, spoke to no one, but all day
Composed his life around the happy scene.

And when the sun went down and keepers came
To lock the gates, and all the voices were
Swept to a distance where no sounds could stir,
This man continued playing his odd game.

Thus, without protest, he went to the gate,
Heard the key turn and shut his eyes until
He felt that he had made the whole place still,
Being content simply to watch and wait.

So one can live, like patterns under glass,
And, like those patterns, not committing harm.
This man continued faithful to his calm,
Watching the children playing on the grass.

But what if someone else should also sit
Beside him on the bench and play the same
Watching and counting, self-preserving game,
Building a world with him no part of it?

If he is truthful to his vision he
Will let the dark intruder push him from
His place, and in the softly gathering gloom
Add one more note to his philosophy.

Father to Son

I do not understand this child
Though we have lived together now
In the same house for years. I know
Nothing of him, so try to build
Up a relationship from how
He was when small. Yet have I killed

82

The seed I spent or sown it where
The land is his and none of mine?
We speak like strangers, there's no sign
Of understanding in the air.
This child is built to my design
Yet what he loves I cannot share.

Silence surrounds us. I would have
Him prodigal, returning to
His father's house, the home he knew,
Rather than see him make and move
His world. I would forgive him too,
Shaping from sorrow a new love.

Father and son, we both must live
On the same globe and the same land.
He speaks: I cannot understand
Myself, why anger grows from grief.
We each put out an empty hand,
Longing for something to forgive.

Warning to Parents

Save them from terror; do not let them see
The ghost behind the stairs, the hidden crime.
They will, no doubt, grow out of this in time
And be impervious as you and me.

Be sure there is a night-light close at hand;
The plot of that old film may well come back,
The ceiling, with its long, uneven crack,
May hint at things no child can understand.

You do all this and are surprised one day
When you discover how the child can gloat
On Belsen and on tortures – things remote
To him. You find it hard to watch him play

With thoughts like these, and find it harder still
To think back to the times when you also
Caught from the cruel past a childish glow
And felt along your veins the wish to kill.

Fears are more personal than we had guessed –
We only need ourselves; time does the rest.

Admonition

Watch carefully. These offer
Surprising statements, are not
Open to your proper doubt,
Will watch you while you suffer.

Sign nothing but let the vague
Slogans stand without your name.
Your indifference they claim
Though the issues seem so big.

Signing a paper puts off
Your responsibilities.
Trust rather your own distress
As in, say, matters of love.

Always behind you, judges
Will have something trite to say.
Let them know you want delay;
No star's smooth at its edges.

The Young Ones

They slip on to the bus, hair piled up high.
New styles each month, it seems to me. I look,
Not wanting to be seen, casting my eye
Above the unread pages of a book.

They are fifteen or so. When I was thus,
I huddled in school coats, my satchel hung
Lop-sided on my shoulder. Without fuss
These enter adolescence; being young

Seems good to them, a state we cannot reach,
No talk of "awkward ages" now. I see
How childish gazes staring out of each
Unfinished face prove me incredibly

Old-fashioned. Yet at least I have the chance
To size up several stages – young yet old,
Doing the twist, mocking an "old-time" dance:
So many ways to be unsure or bold.

A Picture

That dark one in the corner strokes his knife,
Knowing that he can use it if too much
Is asked of him, or if a sudden touch
Shocks him to new awarenesses of life.

The light surrounds the stronger one who fills
The middle distance. Is he thief or saint?
The artist here has shown a bold restraint,
Guessing the hint and not the climax kills.

There is a shadow that he could not find
The colour for. It haunts the picture and
Seems a deliberate gesture of the hand.
But no one saw inside the painter's mind.

A Game of Cards

Determined to be peaceful, we played cards,
Dealt out the hands and hid from one another
Our power. Our only words were weightless words
Like "Your turn", "Thank you" – words to soothe and smother;
Our pulses, slowed to softness, moved together.

So we became opponents and could stare
Like strangers, guessing what the other held.
There was no look of love or passion there.
The pasteboard figures sheltered us, compelled
Each one to win. Love was another world.

And yet within the concentration which
Held us so fast, some tenderness slipped in,
Some subtle feeling which could deftly breach
The kings and queens and prove the pasteboard thin:
Another battle thundered to begin.

A New Pain

When you have gone, I sit and wait, diminished
More than I ever was when quite alone.
Where nothing started, nothing need be finished;
Something of love I learn when you have gone,

Something I never knew before; I mean
The ache, the rending and the dispossession.
When I was quite alone I felt no keen
Edge of the blade, the other side of passion.

Absence becomes almost a presence since
It casts so deep a shadow on my mind:
No trivial lights will comfort or convince,
I lack your way of looking and am blind.

But when you come expectedly, it is
As if more absences than one were cast
Into oblivion. Present ecstasies
Thrive on the very anguish of the past.

A Mental Hospital Sitting-Room

Utrillo on the wall. A nun is climbing
Steps in Montmartre. We patients sit below.
It does not seem a time for lucid rhyming;

Too much disturbs. It does not seem a time
When anything could fertilize or grow.

It is as if a scream were opened wide,
A mouth demanding everyone to listen.
Too many people cry, too many hide
And stare into themselves. I am afraid.
There are no life-belts here on which to fasten.

The nun is climbing up those steps. The room
Shifts till the dust flies in between our eyes.
The only hope is visitors will come
And talk of other things than our disease . . .
So much is stagnant and yet nothing dies.

The Interrogator

He is always right.
However you prevaricate or question his motives,
Whatever you say to excuse yourself
He is always right.

He always has an answer;
It may be a question that hurts to hear.
It may be a sentence that makes you flinch.
He always has an answer.

He always knows best.
He can tell why you disliked your father,
He can make your purest motive seem aggressive.
He always knows best.

He can always find words.
While you fumble to feel for your own position
Or stammer out words that are not quite accurate,
He can always find words.

And if you accuse him
He is glad you have lost your temper with him.
He can find the motive, give you a reason
If you accuse him.

And if you covered his mouth with your hand,
Pinned him down to his smooth desk chair,
You would be doing just what he wishes.
His silence would prove that he was right.

Night Sister

How is it possible not to grow hard,
To build a shell around yourself when you
Have to watch so much pain, and hear it too?
Many you see are puzzled, wounded; few
Are cheerful long. How can you not be scarred?

To view a birth or death seems natural,
But these locked doors, these sudden shouts and tears
Graze all the peaceful skies. A world of fears
Like the ghost-haunting of the owl appears.
And yet you love that stillness and that call.

You have a memory for everyone;
None is anonymous and so you cure
What few with such compassion could endure.
I never met a calling quite so pure.
My fears are silenced by the things you've done.

We have grown cynical and often miss
The perfect thing. Embarrassment also
Convinces us we cannot dare to show
Our sickness. But you listen and we know
That you can meet us in our own distress.

Words from Traherne

'You cannot love too much, only in the wrong way.'

It seemed like love; there were so many ways
Of feeling, thinking, each quite separate.
Tempers would rise up in a sudden blaze,
Or someone coming twitch and shake the heart.

Simply, there was no calm. Fear often came
And intervened between the quick expression
Of honest movements or a kind of game.
I ran away at any chance of passion.

But not for long. Few can avoid emotion
So powerful, although it terrifies.
I trembled, yet I wanted that commotion
Learnt through the hand, the lips, the ears, the eyes.

Fear always stopped my every wish to give.
I opted out, broke hearts, but most of all
I broke my own. I would not let it live
Lest it should make me lose control and fall.

Now generosity, integrity,
Compassion too, are what make me exist,
Yet still I cannot come to terms or try,
Or even know, the knot I must untwist.

Samuel Palmer and Chagall

You would have understood each other well
And proved to us how periods of art
Are less important than the personal
Worlds that each painter makes from mind and heart.

The greatest – Blake, Picasso – move about
In many worlds. You only have one small
Yet perfect place. In it, there is no doubt,
And no deception can exist at all.

Great qualities make such art possible,
A sense of truth, integrity, a view
Of man that fits into a world that's whole,
Those moons, those marriages, that dark, that blue.

I feel a quiet in it all although
The subject and the scenes are always strange.
I think it is that order pushes through
Your images, and so you can arrange

And make the wildest, darkest dream serene;
Landscapes are like still-lives which somehow move,
The moon and sun shine out of the same scene –
Fantastic worlds but all are built from love.

On a Friend's Relapse and Return
to a Mental Clinic

I had a feeling that you might come back,
And dreaded it.
You are a friend, your absence is a lack;
I mean now that

We do not meet outside the hospital:
You are too ill
And I, though free by day, cannot yet call
Myself quite well.

Because of all of this, it was a shock
To find that you
Were really bad, depressed, withdrawn from me
More than I knew.

You ask for me and sometimes I'm allowed
To go and sit
And gently talk to you – no noise too loud:
I'm glad of it.

You take my hand, say odd things, sometimes weep,
And I return
With rational talk until you fall asleep.
So much to learn

Here; there's no end either at second-hand
Or else within
Oneself, or both. I want to understand
But just begin

When something startling, wounding comes again.
Oh heal my friend.

There should be peace for gentle ones, not pain.
Bring her an end

Of suffering, or let us all protest
And realize
It is the good who often know joy least.
I fight against the size

And weight of such a realization, would
Prefer no answers trite
As this; but feeling that I've understood,
I can accept, not fight.

Night Garden of the Asylum

An owl's call scrapes the stillness.
Curtains are barriers and behind them
The beds settle into neat rows.
Soon they'll be ruffled.

The garden knows nothing of illness.
Only it knows of the slow gleam
Of stars, the moon's distilling; it knows
Why the beds and lawns are levelled.

Then all is broken from its fullness.
A human cry cuts across a dream.
A wild hand squeezes an open rose.
We are in witchcraft, bedevilled.

A Depression

She left the room undusted, did not care
To hang a picture, even lay a book
On the small table. All her pain was there –
In absences. The furious window shook
With violent storms she had no power to share.

Her face was lined, her bones stood thinly out.
She spoke, it's true, but not as if it mattered;
She helped with washing-up and things like that.
Her face looked anguished when the china clattered.
Mostly she merely stared at us and sat.

And then one day quite suddenly she came
Back to the world where flowers and pictures grow
(We sensed that world though we were much the same
As her). She seemed to have the power to know
And care and treat the whole thing as a game.

But will it last? Those prints upon her walls,
Those stacks of books – will they soon disappear?
I do not know how a depression falls
Or why so many of us live in fear.
The cure, as much as the disease, appals.

Grove House, Iffley

For Vivien

Your house is full of objects that I prize –
A marble hand, paperweights that uncurl,
Unfolding endlessly to red or blue.
Each way I look, some loved thing meets my eyes,
And you have used the light outside also;
The autumn gilds collections old and new.

And yet there is no sense of *objets d'art*,
Of rarities just valued for their worth.
The handsome objects here invite one's touch,
As well as sight. Without the human heart,
They'd have no value, would not say so much.
Something of death belongs to them – and birth.

Nor are they an escape for anyone.
Simply you've fashioned somewhere that can give
Not titillation, pleasure, but a sense
Of order and of being loved; you've done
What few can do who bear the scars and prints
Of wounds from which they've learnt a way to live.

Caravaggio's 'Narcissus' in Rome

Look at yourself, the shine, the sheer
Embodiment thrown back in some
Medium like wood or glass. You stare,
And many to this gallery come
Simply to see this picture. Clear
As glass it is. It holds the eye
By subject and by symmetry.

Yes, something of yourself is said
In this great shining figure. You
Must have come to self-knowledge, read
Yourself within that image who
Draws every visitor. You made
From gleaming paint that tempting thing –
Man staring at his suffering.

And at his joy. But you stopped where
We cannot pause, merely make sure
The picture took you from the stare,
Fatal within: Chagall or Blake
Have exorcized your gazing for
A meaning that you could not find
In the cold searchings of your mind.

Chinese Art

You said you did not care for Chinese art
Because you could not tell what dynasties
A scroll or bowl came from. "There is no heart"
You said, "Where time's avoided consciously."

I saw your point because I loved you then.
The willows and the horses and the birds
Seemed cold to me; each skilfully laid-on, thin
Phrase spoke like nothing but unpassionate words.

I understand now what those artists meant;
They did not care for style at all, or fashion.

It was eternity they tried to paint,
And timelessness, they thought, must lack all passion.

Odd that just when my feeling need for you
Has gone all wrong, I should discover this.
Yes, but I lack the sense of what is true
Within these wise old artists' skilfulness.

It would be easy now to close again
My heart against such hurt. Those willows show,
In one quick stroke, a lover feeling pain,
And birds escape fast as the brush-strokes go.

Love Poem

There is a shyness that we have
Only with those whom we most love.
Something it has to do also
With how we cannot bring to mind
A face whose every line we know.
O love is kind, O love is kind.

That there should still remain the first
Sweetness, also the later thirst –
This is why pain must play some part
In all true feelings that we find
And every shaking of the heart.
O love is kind, O love is kind.

And it is right that we should want
Discretion, secrecy, no hint
Of what we share. Love which cries out,
And wants the world to understand,
Is love that holds itself in doubt.
For love is quiet, and love is kind.

One Flesh

Lying apart now, each in a separate bed,
He with a book, keeping the light on late,
She like a girl dreaming of childhood,
All men elsewhere – it is as if they wait
Some new event: the book he holds unread,
Her eyes fixed on the shadows overhead.

Tossed up like flotsam from a former passion,
How cool they lie. They hardly ever touch,
Or if they do it is like a confession
Of having little feeling – or too much.
Chastity faces them, a destination
For which their whole lives were a preparation.

Strangely apart, yet strangely close together,
Silence between them like a thread to hold
And not wind in. And time itself's a feather
Touching them gently. Do they know they're old,
These two who are my father and my mother
Whose fire from which I came, has now grown cold?

For Love

I did not know the names of love
And now they have grown few.
When I this way or that behave,
I want the meaning too.
I want the definition when
The feeling starts to go.

"Yes now," "Yes now", or "It has come" –
Lovers have used these names;
But each one thinks he has found some-
thing separate and strange.
In all the lonely darknesses
We think a new truth gleams.

I am worn out with thinking of
The feelings I have had.
Some strange hand seems to grasp my love
And pull it from the bed.
I wait for clear, undreaming nights
And letters now instead.

The Shaking World

Under all this
There is violence.
The chairs, tables, pictures, paper-weights
Are all moving, moving.
You can't see it but they are being carried
Along with currents and continents.
We too are carried (our peace two quarrelling doves)
And nothing, nothing is still.

A Buddhist monk at his most uplifted
High in the Himalayas
Is moved too.
Great wheels of the world bear him round and round.
We have tried to tie the universe to horoscopes
While we whirl between star and star.

The Unknown Child

That child will never lie in me, and you
Will never be its father. Mirrors must
Replace the real image, make it true
So that the gentle love-making we do
Has powerful passions and a parents' trust.

That child will never lie in me and make
Our loving careful. We must kiss and touch
Quietly and watch our own reflexions break
As in a pool that is disturbed. Oh take
My watchful love; there must not be too much

A child lies within my mind. I see
The eyes, the hands. I see you also there,
I see you waiting with an honest care,
Within my mind, within me bodily,
And birth and death close to us constantly.

Shock

Seeing you cry
Is, for me,
Like seeing others die.

You have been changeless, permanent
As the Equator,
Equal to all tides and suns.
Now it is as if you were a volcano
With a shattered crater.

It is elemental – this.
It is like plants budding, animals mating.
There would be fires and stars in a swift kiss,
Your tears are a storm starting.

Gale

There is an inland gale
And I dream of sea-winds and lobsters.
My mind is open to the full
Places, the islands and harbours:

Also to the lonely ones
The far-off wave
Topped by a bird long-since,
Seeming to speak of love.

And of Noah's Ark I dream –
The gentle animals
Two by two still come –
I hear their footfalls.

And last of all the salt
Taste of the sea and spring
So far inland is felt
Stranger than anything.

The Animals' Arrival

So they came
Grubbing, rooting, barking, sniffing,
Feeling for cold stars, for stone, for some hiding-place,
Loosed at last from heredity, able to eat
From any tree or from ground, merely mildly themselves,
And every movement was quick, was purposeful, was proposed.
The galaxies gazed on, drawing in their distances.
The beasts breathed out warm on the air.

No-one had come to make anything of this,
To move it, name it, shape it a symbol;
The huge creatures were their own depth, the hills
Lived lofty there, wanting no climber.
Murmur of birds came, rumble of underground beasts
And the otter swam deftly over the broad river.

There was silence too.
Plants grew in it, it wove itself, it spread, it enveloped
The evening as day-calls died and the universe hushed, hushed.
A last bird flew, a first beast swam
And prey on prey
Released each other
(Nobody hunted at all):
They slept for the waiting day.

Never to See

Never to see another evening now
With that quick openness, that sense of peace
That, any moment, childhood could allow.

Never to see the spring and smell the trees
Alone, with nothing asking to come in
And shake the mind, and break the hour of ease –

All this has gone since childhood began
To go and took with it those tears, that rage.
We can forget them now that we are men.

But what will comfort us in our old age?
The feeling little, or the thinking back
To when our hearts were their own privilege?

It will be nothing quiet, but the wreck
Of all we did not do will fill our lack
As the clocks hurry and we turn a page.

Bonnard

Colour of rooms. Pastel shades. Crowds. Torsos at ease in brilliant baths. And always, everywhere the light.

This is a way of creating the world again, of seeing differences, of piling shadow on shadow, of showing up distances, of bringing close, bringing close.

A way of furnishing too, of making yourself feel at home – and others. Pink, flame, coral, yellow, magenta – extreme colours for ordinary situations. This is a way to make a new world.

Then watch it. Let the colours dry, let the carpets collect a little dust. Let the walls peel gently, and people come, innocent, nude, eager for bed or bath.

They look newmade too, these bodies, newborn and innocent. Their flesh-tints fit the bright walls and floors and they take a bath as if entering the first stream, the first fountain.

A Letter to Peter Levi

Reading your poems I am aware
Of translucencies, of birds hovering
Over estuaries, of glass being spun for huge domes.
I remember a walk when you showed me
A tablet to Burton who took his own life.
You seem close to fragility yet have
A steel-like strength. You help junkies,
You understand their language,
You show them the stars and soothe them.
You take near-suicides and talk to them.
You are on the strong side of life, yet also the brittle,
I think of blown glass sometimes but reject the simile.
Yet about your demeanour there is something frail,
The strength is within, won from simple things
Like swimming and walking.
Your pale face is like an ikon, yet
Any moment, any hour, you break to exuberance,
And then it is our world which is fragile:
You toss it like a juggler.

Any Poet's Epitaph

It does this, I suppose – protects
From the rough message, coarseness, grief,
From the sigh we would rather not hear too much,
And from our own brief gentleness too.

Poetry – builder, engraver, destroyer,
We invoke you because like us
You are the user of words; the beasts
But build, mate, destroy, and at last
Lie down to old age or simply sleep.

Coins, counters, Towers of Babel,
Mad words spoken in sickness too –
All are considered, refined, transformed,
On a crumpled page or a wakeful mind,
And stored and given back – and true.

100

Considerations

Some say they find it in the mind,
A reason why they should go on.
Others declare that they can find
The same in travel, art well done.

Still others seek in sex or love
A reciprocity, relief.
And few, far fewer daily, give
Themselves to God, a holy life.

But poetry must change and make
The world seem new in each design.
It asks much labour, much heartbreak,
Yet it can conquer in a line.

First Evening

(from the French of Rimbaud)

She was half-undressed;
A few indiscreet trees
Threw out their shadows and displayed
Their leaves, cunningly and close.

She sat, half-naked in my chair,
She clasped her hands,
And her small feet shook
Where the floor bends.

I watched, on her lips
And also on her breast
A stray light flutter
And come to rest.

First it was her ankles I kissed;
She laughed gently, and then
Like a bird she sang
Again and again.

Her feet withdrew and,
In an odd contradiction
She said "Stop, do."
Love knows such affliction.

I kissed her eyes.
My lips trembled, so weak.
Then she opened her lips again and said,
"There are words I must speak."

This was too much, too much.
I kissed her breast and, at once,
She was tender to my touch.
She did not withdraw or wince.

Her clothes had fallen aside,
But the great trees threw out their leaves.
I am still a stranger to love,
Yet this was one of my loves.

The Rooks

(from the French of Rimbaud)

When the meadow is cold, Lord, and when
The Angelus is no longer heard,
I beg you to let it come,
This delightful kind of bird –
The rook – and here make its home.
One, many, sweep down from the skies.

Such an odd army – you birds.
You have very strange voices.
Cold winds attack your nests,
Yet come, I implore, as if words
Were your medium. Where the river rests,
Dry and yellow, by Crosses

And ditches, come forward, come
In your thousands, over dear France
Where many are still asleep.

This is truly your home.
Wheel over so that a chance
Traveller may see the deep

Meaning within you all.
Be those who show men their duty,
And also reveal the world's beauty.
You, all of you
(And I know this is true)
Are the dark attendants of a funeral.

You, saints of the sky,
Of the oak tree, of the lost mast,
Forget about those of the spring,
Bring back hope to the lost
Places, to those who feel nothing
But that defeat is life's cost.

Friendship

Such love I cannot analyse;
It does not rest in lips or eyes,
Neither in kisses nor caress.
Partly, I know, it's gentleness

And understanding in one word
Or in brief letters. It's preserved
By trust and by respect and awe.
These are the words I'm feeling for.

Two people, yes, two lasting friends.
The giving comes, the taking ends.
There is no measure for such things.
For this all Nature slows and sings.

A Sonnet

Run home all clichés, let the deep words come
However much they hurt and shock and bruise.
There is a suffering we can presume,
There is an anger, also, we can use;
There are no categories for what I know
Hunted by every touch on memory.
A postcard can produce a heartbreak blow
And sentiment comes seething when I see
A photograph, a Christmas card or some
Association with this loss, this death.
I must live through all this and with no home
But what he was, keep holding on to breath.
Once the stars shone within a sky I knew.
Now only darkness is my sky, my view.

Let Things Alone

You have to learn it all over again,
The words, the sounds, almost the whole language
Because this is a time when words must be strict and new
Not concerning you,
Or only indirectly,
Concerning a pain
Learnt as most people some time or other learn it
With shock, then dark.

The flowers will refer to themselves always
But should not be loaded too much
With meaning from happier days.
They must remain themselves,
Dear to the touch.
The stars also
Must go on shining without what I now know.
And the sunset must simply glow.

Hurt

They do not mean to hurt, I think,
People who wound and still go on
As if they had not seen the brink

Of tears they forced or even known
The wounding thing. I'm thinking of
An incident. I brought to one,

My host, a present, small enough
But pretty and picked out with care.
I put it in her hands with love,

Saying it came from Russia; there
Lay my mistake. The politics
Each of us had, we did not share.

But I am not immune to lack
Like this in others; she just thrust
The present over, gave it back

Saying, "I do not want it." Must
We hurt each other in such ways?
This kind of thing is worse than Lust

And other Deadly Sins because
It's lack of charity. For this,
Christ sweated blood, and on the Cross

When every nail was in its place,
Though God himself, he called as man
At the rejection. On his face

Among the sweat, there must have been
Within the greater pain, the one
A hurt child shows, the look we can

Detect and feel, swift but not gone,
Only moved deeper where the heart
Stores up all things that have been done

And, though forgiven, don't depart.

Beech

They will not go. These leaves insist on staying.
Coinage like theirs looked frail six weeks ago.
What hintings at, excitement of delaying,
Almost as if some richer fruits could grow

If leaves hung on against each swipe of storm,
If branches bent but still did not give way.
Today is brushed with sun. The leaves are warm.
I picked one from the pavement and it lay

With borrowed shining on my Winter hand.
Persistence of this nature sends the pulse
Beating more rapidly. When will it end,

That pride of leaves? When will the branches be
Utterly bare, and seem like something else,
Now half-forgotten, no part of a tree?

Growing

Not to be passive simply, never that.
Watchful, yes, but wondering. It seems
Strange, your world, and must do always, yet
Haven't you often been caught out in dreams

And changed your terms of reference, escaped
From the long rummaging with words, with things,
Then found the very purpose that you mapped
Has moved? The poem leaves you and it sings.

And you have changed. Your whispered world is not
Yours any longer. It's not there you grow.
I tell you that your flowers will find no plot

Except when you have left them free and slow,
While you attend to other things. Do not
Tamper with touching. Others pick, you know.

106

Transformation

Always I trip myself up when I try
To plan exactly what I'll say to you.
I should allow for how my feelings lie
Ready to leap up, showing what is true,

But in a way I never had designed.
How is it you are always ready when
Those linked ideas like beads within my mind
Break from their thread and scatter tears again?

I am amazed, and distances depart,
Words touch me back to quiet. I am free
Who could not guess such misery would start

And stop so quickly, change the afternoon
And, far much more than that, transfigure me.
Trusting myself, I enter night, stars, moon.

To the Core

You have tried so hard to reach the core
Of what you tell us that you think you are.
Friends find you out, mirrors now explore,
Or you yourself, both eyes gripped to a star

Or two defensive eyes you can't stare out,
Feel down your flesh, with careful fingers, thin
As worn-out thoughts, and find the scars of doubt.
You test appearances upon your skin.

Truth tastes strange to you and lips learn warnings.
Are you afraid when you reach out and kiss
The air, your breath accepting every morning's

Terrible trust? We learn all fear in ways
No books describe to us. We must dismiss
All but the ghosts which give back our own gaze.

A Quartet

Four people in a street where houses were
Devoted to their silence. Voices went
Into an argument. The other pair
Looked at each other with a quiet assent.

So speech, so echoes. What were we explaining?
Pitting ourselves against the stars perhaps?
Two did not move, or need a breath-regaining.
Pause meant a stir of love, for us a lapse

In thought. There was no feeling in our speech
Except the easing out to victory.
Tempers were kept. Better if we had each

Been silent, let the other two go off.
There was one lamp, disputing with a tree.
Ideas of ours broke through those looks of love.

Rhetoric

He told us that it mattered how a bird
(Not naming it) should have its wings so taut
That it was watchful always, could be stirred
By all events except the being caught

And caged by us. Bright symbols bubbled then
Out of his mouth, poets handed lines
To prove his feelings. Quiet once again,
He gave me territory, gave me signs.

The need to prove had gone now for a time,
Yet I was not at ease, was shouldered out,
First by the echoes of a verse or rhyme,

Then by these people's quiet dexterity.
I had no need of birds to show my doubt
But searched the night for some simplicity.

Trance

Naked as possible in cities, these
Young look enchanted. Each attentive face
Could shine a god or goddess in the trees
Of a great forest where the roots found place

Long before man. Yes, in this daze of heat,
Stripped bodies could have stepped from anywhere
To anywhere. The street's no more a street
Of houses where the people have to share

The sense of time. Look, naked children run
Into the water, splashing fountains too
Constant for usual days. They have begun

To change before the watchers' eyes and show
How light is palpable, how day is new,
And, strangely, more so in the sunset glow.

In a Garden

When the gardener has gone this garden
Looks wistful and seems waiting an event.
It is so spruce, a metaphor of Eden
And even more so since the gardener went,

Quietly godlike, but, of course, he had
Not made me promise anything, and I
Had no one tempting me to make the bad
Choice. Yet I still felt lost and wonder why.

Even the beech tree from next door which shares
Its shadow with me, seemed a kind of threat.
Everything was too neat and someone cares

In the wrong way. I need not have stood long
Mocked by the smell of a mown lawn, and yet
I did. Sickness for Eden was so strong.

Grapes

Those grapes, ready for picking, are the sign
Of harvest and of Sacrament. Do not
Touch them; wait for the ones who tread the wine,
See Southern air surround that bunch, that knot

Of juice held in. In Winter vines appear
Pitiful as a scarecrow. No one would
Guess from their crippled and reluctant air
That such refreshment, such fermenting could

Come from what seem dry bones left after death.
But, look now, how those pregnant bunches hang,
Swinging upon a pendulum of breath,

Intense small globes of purple till the hour
Of expert clipping comes. There is a pang
In seeing so much fullness change its power.

Among Strangers

Changed by the darkness their indifference shed
Can you be undiminished yet and share
The harmony you find in picture, bed,
In that defiant moth that meets the air

And passes through it and flies on? Can you
Find in the punishings of this no-love
Yourself, the bell your mind which still rings true
As you face what must be well-known enough?

Back to your childhood, are you now before
Any demands? You were not powerless though,
You cried your need out, joining others. Why

Do you divide and count the distance so?
Look, they are harmless and you need not try
To prise their difference open any more.

110

The Quality of Goodness

Brought up perhaps on some quiet wave of sea
When the boat vanishes and surf reclines
And seen from close at hand as suddenly
A figure folded on the sand's designs

And rising, moving inland – so you stare
With a compassionate serenity
And gaze into my moment of despair.
Total decorum and simplicity.

So I survive and step upon the shore
Which you have yielded. No demands are made.
My laughter is not false, there is no more

Deception. I look back at you, return
Your gaze, am calm upon those tide-out sands,
Sea heard and smelt, too distant to discern.

No Rest

Even while I sit and think and see
Patterns around me which my eyes arrange,
Even while battling out of poetry,
I know some rising in me, summon change

And am existing out of literature,
Not among words or papers any more
But moving among freedoms that are pure.
O no I am not artist but restore

All that was there already, only needing
A touch here; I correct but not improve.
Or change the metaphor – say I am weeding

A garden planted on a stair-cased hill.
I climb and pluck and everywhere I move
I feel unsettled but am learning skill.

For the Mind Explorers

What have you done to some of us privately, to perhaps all
    publicly since you have
Taken away our fables, a child's toys, taken and hidden, sometimes
    destroyed them,
Or so it seems, "for our good". What is this "good" that comes
    with no nurses
That a language, a tongue or one imagination require? You have
    lived, acted, written, some of you even
Have prophesied, have thus taken over our old role while we
    stand, gagged, hands tied, in a small cell.
But not for long. We see to that, we confound you by admitting
    you, by letting you

Trespass upon preserves poets once thought theirs alone. We
    do more,
We grant you a dispensation to take away our symbols, but in
    our wakeful nights, since you have now
Taken away at least some of our dreams, we are gentle with
    you, own you and like the
Raiders, but not spoilers, we have always been, we have plundered,
    your found, held coins and
With extreme delicacy, been Midas with what you have done,
    said or thought. So our magnanimity must
Admit its debt to you – no war, no rage, no guilt, only now
    gratitude and a golden gentleness.

Thunder and a Boy
(for T.)

That great bubble of silence, almost tangible quiet was shattered.
    There was no prelude, the huge chords
Broke and sounded timpani over the town, and then lightning,
    first darting, then strong bars
    Taking hold of the sky, taking hold of us as we sank into
    primitive people,
Wondering at and frightened of the elements, forgetting so
    swiftly how naming had once seemed
    To give them into our hands. Not any longer. We were power-
    less now completely.

But today we have risen with the rain and, though it is torrential,
   we believe at moments that we
Still have power over that. We are wrong. Those birds escaping
   through showers show us
   They are more imperial than we are. We shift, talk, doze, look
     at papers,
Though one child is remembering how last night he stood with
   defiance

   And joy at his window and shouted, "Do it again, God, do it
     again!",
Can we say he was less wise than us? We cannot. He acknowledged
   Zeus,
   Thor, God the Father, and was prepared to cheer or dispute
     with any of them.
This afternoon he watches the sky, praying the night will show
   God's strength again
   And he, without fear, feel those drums beating and bursting
   through his defended, invisible mind.

I Feel

I feel I could be turned to ice
If this goes on, if this goes on.
I feel I could be buried twice
And still the death not yet be done.

I feel I could be turned to fire
If there can be no end to this.
I know within me such desire
No kiss could satisfy, no kiss.

I feel I could be turned to stone,
A solid block not carved at all,
Because I feel so much alone.
I could be grave-stone or a wall.

But better to be turned to earth
Where other things at least can grow.
I could be then a part of birth,
Passive, not knowing how to know.

113

Bird Study

A worm writhes and you have some power
Of knowing when and where to strike.
Then suddenly bread in a shower.
Being a bird is like

This and a feathered overcoat,
A throb of sound, a balanced wing,
A quiver of the beak and throat,
A gossip-mongering.

But higher up a hawk will take
Stature of stars, a comet-fall,
Or else a swan that oars a lake,
Or one note could be all.

I am obsessed with energy
I never touch. I am alive
To what I only hear and see,
The sweep, the sharp, the drive.

Towards a Religious Poem

Decrees of a dead tongue gone,
The flicker of Greek in the vernacular,
An age for the East and Yoga,
For lotus and resting. One word
Cannot be spoken or carved.
If music suggests it, it erred.
Christ in this age you are nameless,
Your praises and slanders have sunk
To oaths. Love has somehow slipped by
What once throbbed in an occupied sky.

In my stanzas I'll only allow
The silence of a tripped tongue,
The concerns and cries of creation
To hold you, as always, but more now.
The Prophets and all their books prosper,

But here as a Christmas comes closer,
Awe will be speechless, and magic
Be dropped like an acrobat's pitfall.
The absence, the emptiness echo,
A girl with a cradle to borrow.

After a Time

(for a friend dead two years)

I have not stood at this grave nor have I
Been where men come at last to silence when
Death sends them to instinctive ceremony,
Whether in torturing sun or fitting rain,
Whether they stare or cry.

What do I say who never put a wreath
Down for a father or this friend? Someone
Will make the speech for me. O this dear death,
Two years of missing all have been undone,
Yet I am growing with

Spontaneous strengths, blessings I did not claim –
Laughter, a child, knowledge of justice and
Faith like a cross which oddly bears my name,
Falls round my neck. In early hours I stand
Reflecting how I came

To this. What takes me through the corridors
Of grief? Was it the touch of love, that leading thread
Which drew me to glad grief from wrong remorse,
Wiped off the dust and let me see the dead
With new care now, new laws?

The Lord's Prayer

"Give us this day." Give us this day and night.
Give us the bread, the sky. Give us the power
To bend and not be broken by your light.

115

And let us soothe and sway like the new flower
Which closes, opens to the night, the day,
Which stretches up and rides upon a power

More than its own, whose freedom is the play
Of light, for whom the earth and air are bread.
Give us the shorter night, the longer day.

In thirty years so many words were spread,
And miracles. An undefeated death
Has passed as Easter passed, but those words said

Finger our doubt and run along our breath.

Meditation on the Nativity

All gods and goddesses, all looked up to
And argued with and threatened. All that fear
Which man shows to the very old and new –
All this, all these have gone. They disappear
In fables coming true,

In acts so simple that we are amazed –
A woman and a child. He trusts, she soothes.
Men see serenity and they are pleased.
Placating prophets talked but here are truths
All men have only praised

Before in dreams. Lost legends here are pressed
Not on to paper but in flesh and blood,
A promise kept. Her modesties divest
Our guilt of shame as she hands him her food
And he smiles on her breast.

Painters' perceptions, visionaries' long
Torments and silence, blossom here and speak.
Listen, our murmurs are a cradle-song,
Look, we are found who seldom dared to seek –
A maid, a child, God young.

Christ on the Cross

Forgive them, Father, forgive them Father who
Is in my heart. How frightened she who stands,
My mother with my friend. The soldiers too,
Help me forgive them who have nailed my hands.
It seems so long ago

I talked in Temples. O the streams where John,
Another, poured the fountain on my head.
Father, I tell my mother that a son,
My friend, shall care for her when I am dead.
I am so dizzy on

This wood. The waters flow but now from me.
I have been chosen. Father, I am you
Who breathed, then sapped the great man-offered tree.
Spirit within me, there are risings too.
Father, forgive now, me.

Easter Duties

They are called duties. People must confess,
Through garlic-smelling grilles or in quiet rooms,
All the year's mis-events – unhelped distress,
Griefs lingered over, *accidie* in dreams,
And hear the words which bless

And unbind, eat the bread and feel the cross
Hurting only a little, hinting more.
Why do I feel, in all these acts, a loss,
As if a marvel I had waited for
Were a cheap toy to toss

Away, the giver gone? Why do I care
In this uncaring? I need gods on earth,
The wonder felt, sleep which I somehow share
Because it is a going back to birth.
And, yes, I want to bear

117

Anticipated laughter, jokes which once
Meant calibre and bite but did not make
Anyone sad. Prayer yet could be a dance
But still a cross. I offer small heartbreak,
Catch grace almost by chance.

Whitsun Sacrament

Others anoint. But you choose your own name.
This comes with childhood just about to leave.
It comes with new self-consciousness, old shame,
Arrives when we are not sure we believe.
We read about a flame

And answers when we question every word,
Mumble our motives. Spirit, Spirit, where
Are you to be caught now and where be heard?
We only feel the pitched-low, taunting air.
There was talk of a bird,

A dove. Where is peace now in our unrest –
The childish questions in the throbbing mind,
The new name, itching loins, the shaping breast?
When we most need a tongue we only find
Christ at his silentest.

Out of the Heights

Out of the preening and impetuous heights
Where we look down and do not fear and risk
The snow escaping, the ice-melting flights,

And where we spin the sun a golden disc
And do not care and watch the clouds attend
The tall sky's dazzling and arched arabesque,

Out of those places where we think we end
Unhappiness, catch love within a final hand,
God, from such places keep us and defend

The innocence we do not understand,
The darknesses to which we must descend.

The Nature of Prayer

(a debt to Van Gogh's "Crooked Church")

Maybe a mad fit made you set it there
Askew, bent to the wind, the blue-print gone
Awry, or did it? Isn't every prayer
We say oblique, unsure, seldom a simple one,
Shaken as your stone tightening in the air?

Decorum smiles a little. Columns, domes
Are sights, are aspirations. We can't dwell
For long among such loftiness. Our homes
Of prayer are shaky and, yes, parts of Hell
Fragment the depths from which the great cry comes.

Thomas Aquinas

Thinking incessantly, making cogitations always but as keenly,
    freshly as the child
He had been who asked repeatedly "What is God?" and was
    pursued by this inquiry till grown-up,
And family factions argued, as they thought logically, that he
Must be an Abbot, they had long doomed this – he, Thomas of
    Aquin, then revolted, but typically
    Mildly and unviolently. No aristocracy for him but in ideas
    and he had settled his destiny to be
A Dominican friar. The one act of outrage we know of is when
    Relations sent in women to tempt his body and he drove them
    out with a

Burning brand. After that, Albert to instruct him, Plato read
and discarded, then
Aristotle transformed with clarity into a great system coinciding
with every
Christian dogma, dancing metaphysical thought, and he put
down calmly the ending in
The Summa for students, for others more and deeper, if possible,
matters.
And he, who patterned and explained the world, dined with
Louis of France, still
Stayed the child of great questions, saint but like an angel, and
rightly, now
Known among us as the Angelic Doctor, a Church's title for one
whose sole wish was for the pure gold of continual inquiry.

Open to the Public

They fall in easy poses as if they
    Knew the sun's moods by heart,
Expected it, as in hot lands. Each day
    They soon become a part

Of the stretched grass unmown where shining flowers
    Stare straight into the light.
Grown-ups and children all accept its powers
    As if it were a right.

They are adaptable to changes, so
    Here where the sun can bruise
With brightness where they bask, they all still know
    This climate is for use.

Yet they are not complacent. Watch them run
    Fast when the sun comes out
And for a moment shrug fore-knowledge. Sun
    Is strong before all doubt.

In a Picture Gallery

Show me a gallery of air
And walls shored up with paintings through
Which we can climb. A step, a stair
Takes us to sunsets or a view
Of light sufficient to a square
Of harlequinning people who

Set minds to music. Do you hear
A murmur of continued flight?
Paint, sound and word are everywhere,
A quick kaleidoscope of light.
Are paintings far or are we near
This texture of, this sound of sight?

Mondrian

Attempt a parody of this:
Prepare the paints, make measurements,
Keep an eye cocked on memory,
Call up geometry, stand back,
Extend the rainbow's ready scope.

But Mondrian will not appear.
He starves still with an easel too
Heavy to hang on, fever high,
Caught too late with canvases
For barter in the auction rooms.

Can abstractions tell the tale?
Are portraits put in angles, squares?
Still life, still death and one thing more –
The dignity of distances,
The lofty white a man's last breath.

Rembrandt's Late Self-Portraits

You are confronted with yourself. Each year
The pouches fill, the skin is uglier.
You give it all unflinchingly. You stare
Into yourself, beyond. Your brush's care
Runs with self-knowledge. Here

Is a humility at one with craft.
There is no arrogance. Pride is apart
From this self-scrutiny. You make light drift
The way you want. Your face is bruised and hurt
But there is still love left.

Love of the art and others. To the last
Experiment went on. You stared beyond
Your age, the times. You also plucked the past
And tempered it. Self-portraits understand,
And old age can divest,

With truthful changes, us of fear of death.
Look, a new anguish. There, the bloated nose,
The sadness and the joy. To paint's to breathe,
And all the darknesses are dared. You chose
What each must reckon with.

Mozart's Horn Concertos

Not for war or hunting cry
Is this; it gentles down the heart,
So there's no question asking "Why

Does man exist?" God gave him art,
And God is proved in every note
And every sound takes its own part

In what a young composer wrote
Who ended in a pauper's grave.
The disc is on, the patterns float

And I feel back at some strange start
And marvel at what Mozart gave.

A Scholar Emperor of the Tang Dynasty

Dazzling it was indeed, a golden age,
The lakes ran round the palaces, the park
Was, yes, a turned, illuminated page.
    You did not think of dark

Or only as a time when candles curled
Over a manuscript and filled the air
With pens, with eyes to circumscribe the world,
    And you were moving there,

No autocrat but patron till a strong
And swarming dynasty took off your power,
Put you in exile. Poetry, the long
    Finger of time, its hour,

Gave you the diffidence and dared you look
At moon-extending shadows, short-lived sun.
You also added letters to a book
    But now a home-sick one.

Wasn't it worth it? Didn't all those days
Of letting others write and paint allow
This gift of loss, lament which felt like praise
    And proves it is so now?

Wonder

(Homage to Wallace Stevens)

Wonder exerts itself now as the sky
Holds back a crescent moon, contains the stars.
So we are painters of a yesterday
Cold and decisive. We are feverish
With meditations of a Winter Law
Though Spring was brandished at us for a day.

Citizens of climate we depend
Not on the comfortable clock, the warm
Cry of a morning song, but on the shape
Of hope, the heralding imagination,
The sanguine making and the lonely rites
We exercise in space we leave alone.

Prophets may preside and they will choose
Clouds for a throne. The background to their speech
Will be those fiery peaks a painter gives
As a composer shares an interval,
As poet pauses, holding sound away
From wood, as worshippers draw back from gods.

A Chinese Sage

A Chinese sage once took every word distilled, altered and
    perfected
In private till for him it seemed a poem, yes he took this to a
    peasant woman,
    Read it to her softly and slowly and waited for her rough-voiced
    assurance that
Certain words she could understand, others were meaningless
    to her. Very discreetly
    But decisively, and with no arguments, this sage crossed out
    every word that was foreign to
A woman of simplicity who knew labours of the soil and the
    house, who had no
    Dealings other than this with poetry, art of any kind, yet by his

    Magnanimity, more, his humility, became his mentor, guided
    him
Out of all obscurity, not with wearying argument or even quiet
    coaxing, but by the fact
    That she was a world he could only enter through her. Hay,
    beds, crude meals, lust
Subdued his wit, bodied out his verse, cancelled cleverness. And,
    I ask, was he

Most poet or most philosopher in this uncrowned wisdom, writing
In the reign of Charlemagne, paring simplicities to a peace no
  Emperor was ever enticed by or even dreamed of?

Elegy for W.H. Auden

Stones endure as your first and last things.
The carpet slippers, the leather skin,
The incorrigible laughter inaccurately aped,

Those late epigrams which obviously were
The acute desperation of that laughter –
These are forgotten almost already.

But the stone your student hand held gently,
Schoolboy hair flopped over years later,
The limestone which reminded you of love

And caught the last strains of your lyrical perceptions,
The walks out of Italy into Austria,
All that grey North which you set glowing –

Yes, it is geology, quarries and tools,
The precise tap on the finished fossil,
And last the shuffle on Christ Church cobbles,

The cobbles you must have stared at rather
Than look up as Wren's Tom trembled your hours –
All these are a life you refused to surrender.

No glass-cases and no museums.
All your grand operas opened into caves
Where your Orators shout and your Mirror is shining.

The Sea stands still but your landscape moves.

Prospero

All back into their places, steps
Printed on sand, and air to air
Confides, great fruit from spent trees drops.
O Prospero, how you prepare

And ravish in the giving back,
Lamb to the ewe, isle to the sea
And Ariel self-swung and quick
In that good hour of setting free.

Hopkins in Wales

We know now how long that language,
Your language, had been dancing in you but
    Suppressed, held back by hard work, the debt
You owed to discipline. But no one, not one
    Stopped you looking, dissecting at a glance
A leaf, a tree's stump, while in your mind
    The long thought-over, now fermented
Ideas of Duns Scotus were waiting, the vintage
    Years about to be bottled at one sign, a word
From a Superior about the wreck you had read of.
    Worked-out ideas, your "instress" and "inscape",
Problems of prosody, "Sprung Rhythm", came out dancing,
    Linked with that subject, and you wrote at last

    Guiltless, no squabble now between your vocation,
Endurance chosen as a priest, with art, two arts
    Now stretching within you with all the force of
Deliberations held back. And the discipline itself
    Appeared in selected stanzas, half-rhymes, senses once
        subdued
Unleashed into another order. A nun, a shipwreck
    Were set down, had happened but now would happen
Over and over in the committed, inexorable, also defenceless
    Way in which poems are always vulnerable. And every long
        look

126

At a leaf's individuality or the mark, his own, on a man's face
  Was dynamic. And the heroism heard of
Found place with all your admirations, while God's Presence
  Was granted a new kind of immanence in your lines. Doubtless

The no-understanding of others hurt but, far deeper
  And like the sea you wrote of, the fitness,
Inexorably of this exercise and joy, flowered in you, jetsam
  To others in time, acknowledged by you and by us
Years later. Let us hope you had some inkling of this
  As you rode through so many other poems until Dublin
Felled you like an axe or a wave into
  A desirable death, your work around you
Careful as carved stones simply waiting to be picked up,
  Wondered at, not static but dynamically precious,
Named by you, found by us, never diminishing.

Performer

    Tight-roper, care, do not look down,
    Think of the thread beneath your foot,
    Forget the pony and the clown,
    Discard the circus, see before
    Your gaze a safety held, complete
    And, after that, the tidal roar

    Of watchers, some of whom no doubt
    Wanted a death. You have an hour
    When you can cast your terror out,
    Depend no more on balance but
    On earth whose ground gives you the power,
    You think, to snatch that rope and cut.

A Play at Avignon

    Emptiness after midnight since the voices
    Had stopped at last, no echo left behind
      Within that courtyard. Stars had crowded out
    Sound, and because there had been voices once

There was a vacancy that almost, now,
Seemed to be measurable. The actors had
　Spoken their classic lines and simply bowed
And moved from sight. Day would redeem the view,
　The famous broken bridge turn thoughts to rivers
Or else to painting. Southern atmosphere,
　Pervasive and imprisoning, would return

And pick each small square out, each watered field,
Light point the way to Orange or to Nîmes,
　And all Provence be like a text of which
You know the language, linger on the page
　And hear the voices speaking in your mind
Different from those within the palace of
　Disputed Popes. So Avignon arranges
Itself and seen from any point you choose,
　Softens and ripens as the day proceeds
Never preparing you but letting happen
　Those voices, the whole city slipped from sight.

Opera

　These lovers must rely
On the adjustment of the wood and strings
Which, in their turn, are guided by
　The baton beating down the air.
Italian, French or German rings
Towards the fatal hour. The theatre

　Is words subjected to
The stretch and fling of sound. Poets withdraw
Or let their rhythms here subdue
　Themselves. Meanings also demur
Without poetic justice, law.
Yet it is this subjection that can stir

　Us by a story which
Climbs out of farce into high tragedy,
Love thrives upon the rich

128

Deceptions winnowing the ear,
While instruments and voices free
Us to rejoicing pain and apt despair.

After a Play

The wind in spasms swept the street
As we walked very quietly
Till cold and silence seemed to meet
And make one point – one star set free
Between two stormy clouds. We leant
Upon both wind and words we meant.

A tense and joyful audience had
Thronged in the theatre we left.
Lovers had laughed at being sad
And justice, mercy were bereft
Of all abstractions. So were we,
Talking so low yet passionately.

Creators in Vienna

That dance we have heard of, so far back now that
We do not know who first pushed it gently into
    A child's mind. But Vienna, Vienna, no mere tapping
In rooms or pavements. Ideas were dancing also, especially in
    Four men's minds, ideas to change us, linking and breaking
Like dancers. The other two, a painter, a philosopher.
    Four kings crowned now by decades of acceptance,

Two trying to heal – Freud, Adler leaping down our
Apparently never-before-discovered minds, entering our dreams,
    Telling us of love and power, changing love and power,
And Kokoschka painting and enriching, purifying, disclosing,
    Wittgenstein quietly challenging centuries of speculation.
                                    They are moving, moving still
These men, they pursue us. Time out of mind we
    Check them, deny. As we do they smile at us because

Our queries continually prove them right, their power
Is no Prospero-wand. They have discarded nothing at all
    For our minds are brimmed with their voices, our hearts
Dance differently now. We are spellbound. We are islands.
    Madness has been given order, painting pours out on posterity.
The thinker, as always, is pressed dry between two pages some-
    where
    Of a book containing the world, a book which can never be
    written.

Orpheus

Not looking back, not looking back –
For him that was the test. We have,
    All of us, camped out, somewhere, some time
In a place, underground or in full sunlight,
    Where we must choose. So our myths later
Instruct us, and our beliefs, whether in Eden
    Or oblivion, take for granted free-will,
Act on that assumption, even in unbelieving.

Thus Orpheus running through Hades with
A lyre so enchantable once, was himself
    Now enchained. That girl, she must, could be his.
But he must not look back. He saw light,
    A little like Lazarus, with the same trust,
The same astonishment, but for him life was behind
    In that place there. Misjudging the threshold
Or perhaps forgetting the promise, he turned, stunned,
    Seeing only darkness, no lyre could call her back, the girl
Had gone, the gods dealt out their punishment.

Persephone

For Spring and Summer she appeared and was
Blinded at first by light. To us she meant
Autumn and Winter were away because
For those two seasons she retreated, went

Back to the dark world, darker than our own.
When she arrived the petals opened to
Welcome her with their wreaths, twine round her throne.
Birds hatched their eggs and all things richly grew.

She went away quite silently one night.
The air was cold next day. From every tree
Leaves fell in dusty disarray to light
And burn the shadow of Persephone.

Snake Charmer

The body writhes and rounds. The fingers feel
A circle, find a note. Up from the ground
Rears the caught serpent. It unwinds its coil
And dances to the sound

The player blows. His eyes address those eyes.
He is the choreographer who's made
The pattern of the dance, its length and size.
Danger is what is played.

In jeopardy, in thrall, the watchers can't
Help moving to the creature which they fear.
But they are safe as long as music's sent
Though that's not what they hear.

This is a rite but this is power also.
It happens now, yet enterprises such
As this take timid men to long ago
When the first reed's first touch

Haunted a jungle, hypnotised a snake.
This is no charming, this is courage when
At any moment faulty notes can break
Out anarchy again.

The Minotaur

Daedalus designed this. Famous for buildings he did Minos'
   will. Minos, full of revenge, yet could not
Kill this creature begotten by his wife and a bull coupling. Poseidon
   punished him in this way,
   Making for us a pattern as perfect and intricate as that labyrinth.
We want the danger, the escape, above all
We want a happy love story to cancel a passion which was prodigal
   only of
A half-bull. Ariadne waited on this, patient as Penelope. She
   had seen the handsome Athenians one by one
Go into Daedalus' design and die there. But she possessed joyfully
   the power of a thread and a secret.

At first sight, as even classical writers will show and allow us,
   she fell in love with Theseus who arrived
Apparently just a victim. But she, and we want this too, always
   this necessity and ceremony,
   Gave him the thread, the clue, the condition to be his wife.
Theseus, quick with courage and passion,
Took the twine from her, smiled and walked into the darkness
   watchfully but fearlessly and found
The Minotaur sleeping. Beautiful indeed but now to be beaten
   to death by young fists, exalted
In no bull-ring with panoply but providing us with the desired
   peril before love succeeds,
   Leading us gently into labyrinths within us where half-bulls
   sometimes wake in our own darkness
And where we must always all be both Theseus and Ariadne.

Not Abstract

Where the river bends, where the bridges break,
Where the willow does not quite
Fall to the current – here is the place to stake
Your life in, your delight
Once easily lost. Here again you could make
A day out of half a night.

The moon is assured. The sun has put its back
Against the wood, the trees
Carry their rotten fruit like a swollen sack.
Stand among all of these
And learn from desertion and luxurious lack
Why some fall on their knees.

Gods have given. Gods have taken away
But left us with the need,
In angry arguments, logics which pray
Even for ghosts of a creed.
The bridge is broken and the willows sway.
Where does the river lead?

Little Peace

Through intricacy of sharp air
The urgent messages are sent.
Voices become a thoroughfare,
Crunched leaves are now irrelevant.

For seasons have resigned to let
Emergencies take on the sway
Where rules and governments once met
And legal systems drew each day

A quiet map, imposed a scheme
For living through. Now to exist
Through hours that shake men from a dream
Makes them take care not to be missed.

For not appearing will put them
In cells unwardered and unbarred.
Strange that a child still shouts its game
And has not heard the times are hard.

Trees shake, leaves drop. But who will win
Such trembling apprehensions warred
Where blood runs cold, blood-sheds begin,
That child ignoring and ignored?

Because huge violence is a threat,
A few are frenzied to be kind,
Warm one another yet, and yet
Hope is still hunted. Who will find?

Spy

The cleaving currents of dispute
Hold back. The vengeances now lie
With a few batteries of loot,
While a consenting, unhelped spy

Is wary, wondering what to do.
There may be armistice. He does
Not know the false reports from true
But waits in hiding. Is his cause

Or what he thought a war proclaimed
Ended? How long can he last out,
Starving now simply to be named,
Despair itself a thread of doubt?

Prisoner

Feel up the walls, waters ooze. The cold
Cranes down the spine. The wayward sky won't fit
A window, a square, but a square equates itself
With the eye in the brain, in the nervous system. All
Which flesh becomes without food and a little water.

I am tired. The planet curves, I cannot sleep.
How many moons have shone in how many shapes?
I am wistful in wisdom, honest in rich endearments,
Hollow perhaps, a channel for any whisper.
The long night takes my loneliness into its hands.

Behind All Iron Curtains

Ambassadors were dignified and curt
And even whispered in brocaded halls.
The slightest emphasis made someone start.
Meanwhile, pent anger hid behind the walls.

Answers were easy. It was questions which
Sent the eyes darting and the eyelids down.
One secretary slipped out of this reach,
Preferring all the tumult of the town.

Two wanted to make love but could not find
A room, a park, even a pool of shadow.
There was a haunting in the loving mind
And every mother seemed to be a widow.

One boy went out alone. There was a hush
Of people disappearing, then, far-off
A better tone, the beating, tidal rush.

He stood as though a statue in a hot
Strewn-with-siesta square. He heard a cough.
Smiling, he turned and, with a smile, was shot.

Happenings

Some say contentious Summers drove them to
A mountain range where they could touch the ice.
Then feel the finger-tip of thawing twice
When the hot cities cried "Our need is you."

Others were stunned awake, their mouths were sand
Choking, their spread of skin felt like a shore
Whose sweat was tides which only can withdraw.
They woke from this to lineaments of land.

And a forsaken few, who found forsaking
A suffering that pleased them with its skill,
Worked out proud plots their dreams could not fulfil
Though the beginnings had been so breath-taking.

135

Some kindly quiet ones were swept away
Until their own compassion cried "Be mild."
Madness caught up and set a mask that smiled
On such domestic, dutiful dismay.

Twelve great imaginations disappeared
Till someone's memory went deeply down
And grasped a goodness which they gave a crown.
Part of the world for two hours was not feared.

Visions and revolutions such as these
Are trusted to no treasure-hunts but lie
Beneath an unportending birdless sky
Waiting for, O, what men, what histories?

Not for Use

A little of Summer spilled over, ran
In splashes of gold on geometry slates.
The grass unstiffened to pressure of sun.
I looked at the melting gates

Where icicles dropped a twinkling rain,
Clusters of shining in early December,
Each window a flaring, effulgent stain.
And easy now to remember

The world's for delight and each of us
Is a joy whether in or out of love.
'No one must ever be used for use,'
Was what I was thinking of.

Wishes

I hired a boat and told the sailors to
Take me to a hot island where the palms
Give you warm breath, and on the sands a few
Shells wait to be wrapped up in the sea's arms.

I begged a lonely man to show me where
A desert and a mirage might be found
And some oasis would give quenching air
As water blossomed from the ancient ground.

I asked some lovers if they knew the way
To some old friends of mine. They did not know;
They had not even heard the time of day.
The sunlight seemed to make their bodies glow.

I asked a priest where he had found his God.
He handed me a musty-smelling book.
I stared into his eyes and thought it odd
That he should have such an untrustful look.

I asked a child if he could cross the road
Safely. He did not speak but took my hand.
The shaking traffic seemed to shift my load
But there were thoughts I longed to understand.

Ends

A city afraid of its darknesses,
Stone and wood and creeper wore
Their fitful mourning. An odd or even
Light appealed with a tiny gesture.
People ashamed of the cold they hide.

It could be the end of the world. It could
Be the almost last moment. Yes, there might
Have been a warning, men given a chance
To collect together their better feelings,
Create a contrition just in time.

We did not think it would be like this.
We imagined thunder-bolts or a blaze
Of all the stars colliding and clinging,
The moon head on to the sun. And so
It well may be. This is not the end.

In spite of the shame, in face of the fear
Half a cleaned Classical column withstood
The thriving moon which must increase.
Marching clouds were packing the sky
And one or two or three stepped clear.

Particular

Milk is on rocks, sea is only
Faintly tidal. The same sail draws
Its red sheet on a washing blue.
A telescope picks out rocks.
Limpets cling to their fastness.

Somebody's photograph? It wasn't.
Geologist's playground? No.
A scene unglossed by sentiment.
No one has ever been there.

A slice of an island this is.
The hem of a dream held fast.
Immaculate invitation.
A move towards innocence.

A place revered so richly
Is untampered as the moon.
But idylls are earmarked always
And we have set our seal

On the power which pulls a particular
Sea. This fragment of shore
Was sand-castled once by a child
But isn't now any more.

Childhood in Lincolnshire

Six years of a flat land.
Grasses cut your fingers on that shore.
People kept calling it Holland and a child

Thought this on some map somewhere
Linked it with that place
A Dutch doll came from.
So the sea trafficked with imagination
Which was more luminous even
Than the blazing tulips in formidable ranks
Or honeysuckle,
The first flower to be seen and smelt,
Tied to its own event and potent for that, therefore, always.

Losing and Finding

You had been searching quietly through the house
That late afternoon, Easter Saturday,
And a good day to be out of doors. But no,
I was reading in a north room. You knocked
On my door once only, despite the dark green notice,
"Do not disturb". I went at once and found you,

Paler than usual, not smiling. You just said
"I've lost them". That went a long way back
To running, screaming through a shop and knocking
Against giants. "I haven't had lunch", you said.
I hadn't much food and the shop was closed for Easter
But I found two apples and washed them both for you.

Then we went across the road, not hand in hand.
I was wary of that. You might have hated it
And anyway you were talking and I told you
About the river not far off, how some people
Swam there on a day like this. And how good the grass
Smelt as we walked to the Recreation Ground.

You were lively now as I spun you lying flat,
Talking fast when I pushed you on the swing,
Bold on the chute but obedient when, to your question
About walking up without hands, I said "Don't. You'll fall".
I kept thinking of your being lost, not crying,
But the sense of loss ran through me all the time

You were chatting away. I wanted to keep you safe,
Not know fear, be curious, love people
As you showed me when you jumped on my lap one evening,
Hugged me and kissed me hard. I could not keep you
Like that, contained in your joy, showing your need
As I wished *I* could. There was something elegiac

Simply because this whole thing was direct,
Chance, too, that you had found me when your parents
So strangely disappeared. There was enchantment
In the emptiness of that playground so you could
Be free for two hours only, noted by me, not you.
An Easter Saturday almost gone astray

Because you were lost and only six years' old.
And it was you who rescued me, you know.
Among the swings, the meadow and the river,
You took me out of time, rubbed off on me
What it feels like to care without restriction,
To trust and never think of a betrayal.

An Event

Legs in knee-socks,
Standing on the rough playground,
Suddenly thinking, "Why am I here?"

No one else seemed near you,
Though they had been, still were
Except for this awareness.

Long before adolescence
This happened, happened more than once.
Is this the onset

Of that long-travelling,
Never answered
Question, "Who am I?"

It could be.
The state does not last
But the memory does.

And soon the shouts surround you again.
You have a blue and a red marble in your hand.
It is your turn to roll one.

Need

Only you would notice what lay under
The practised smile, the just not jumping nerve.
You would have known this was a hint of thunder
To break out later. Yes, you would observe

The manners learnt yet meaning nothing now
But "Let's pretend." You've seen my nursery,
Sifted the pleasure from the grief, shown how

I need not act. The irony, you know,
Is when I'm with you I enjoy the part
Of playing someone else, put selves on show

Simply because I need not. I don't fit
Either the worn-out or the tempted heart.
Tell me the words to feel the truth of it.

Accepted

You are no longer young,
Nor are you very old.
There are homes where those belong.
You know you do not fit
When you observe the cold
Stares of the old who sit

In bath-chairs or the park
(A stick, then, at their side),
Or find yourself in the dark

141

And see the lovers who,
In love and in their stride,
Don't even notice you.

This is a time to begin
Your life. It could be new.
The sheer not fitting in
With the old who envy you
And the young who want to win,
Not knowing false from true,

Means you have liberty
Denied to their extremes.
At last now you can be
What the old cannot recall
And the young long for in dreams,
Yet still include them all.

An Abandoned Palace

A palace where the courtiers have vanished fleetly because
The work was too hard, and where they squabbled continually
    about their rights
And the Queen's debt to them – this has foundered as if the
    close sea had
Rolled over and entered the doors. People ran out screaming.
    Two stayed – an old woman bound to rheumatic fingers and
    the now hard
Embroidery she insisted on finishing. The other was the undeposed
    but rejected and
Uncomplaining Queen, who did not mind that the crown was
    covered
With mildew, the jewels were sold. She was subdued into a soft,
    slow,
Ever-expanding melancholy, though her eyes smiled,
Bidding farewell to the servants gone, asking only that
    The steward should remain, add up the valuables and
Sell them. Then, in the high bedroom, she sat thinking

Of utter simplicities, the heir who had gone to travel the world
    and had not
Written. In her note-book she wrote two words only, two words
    Of disfigured defiance meaning almost total loss. The words
        were
    "Find me." Quickly she took a moulting carrier pigeon to trust
        this message to
    And, with careful hands, glided the bird out of the tarnished
        windows and then
Sat, waiting, occasionally visiting the trembling old woman,
    admiring
    The progress of the stitching, herself hiding tears, still, some-
        how, hoping for
Rescue, reprieve, an escape from a palace now a prison where
    hope itself
    Taunted her continually with its expert disappointments,
Its refusal to gaze back at her long, caught in its own desperate
    incapacity.

Rather Like a Peacock

You say you saw a bird much like a peacock,
Not proud of its own plumage, powerless with it
And being like a beacon to all comers,
Bedraggled birds, small but with the sharp
Anger and strength that comes when brightness is

Discerned, observed as dangerous, a threat
Simply by being passively attractive.
Yes, but among that gathering of birds,
Helpless, you said it was, and vulnerable.
Beaks bit into the colours and you thought

Of other creatures, human beings who
Have gifts not so flamboyant yet observed,
Envied. Tormentors, tireless as those birds,
Sense there's a threat, that here is something which
Might change their lives if given freedom, so,

They, who are quick at this thing only, find
The weak spot and with hostile words and looks
Darken that dazzle, rid themselves of fear
By forcing it upon the one they won't
Dare let it bring its brilliance to their minds.

What happened to that bird within your garden,
Target upon your turf? Could you scare off
Those small attackers, or were you too late?
Can you suggest a safe place for the being
Harassed just here, alive, alert, laid open?

Given Notice
(for Clare)

It was the going back which gathered
A pack of thoughts, feelings also.
They spilt from my hands as I looked about.
A window which held contentment once
Framed a sky unfit for viewing,
But the grey of it fell with glare enough

On squat chessmen, a kaleidoscope,
A Russian bear, an Italian mug.
The full and flare of the place were rich,
But I in the middle of it was mute
Begging within myself for one,

Yes just one day and a different sky.
How hot I became with remembrances,
Then a feather of fear with strength enough
To connect the subtle silences,
Unhoard discourses valued now.

The room was an animal money-box
Smashed in pieces, the coins thrown down.
It was that returning which did it all,
Unlodged the losses I'd thought well-hidden –
People who came or did not come,

The bird outside which seemed to stick
On a single branch through a keepsake June
Of pell-mell skies and unscathed stars,
Broken yet holding petals and leaves,
All too much outside and within.

You who had never been before
Watched my wistfulness, saw the shrug,
Contained the sigh in a silence shared.
Toys are terrible, rooms are let
As blood is sometimes, for transfusion.

Leaving a Room

Somebody said "Like an amputation,"
Another, "Part of your character."
Both were right: growing and breaking,
The nine, nineteen, nine hundred lives
Have been breathed in minutes, hours and weeks here
Eighteen months by the calendar.
I have put both anchor and roots down.

My seasons were torn off a Summer layered
With raiding sunsets; bonfires blew
Away before me. Pictures faded
Slightly. I bronzed, slightly also.
What a litter of life I have crowded here,
What a residue of authentic gold!
I cannot keep it now.

The gallery, toyshop, study stand.
Clocks are striking round me, pendula
Pursue their energy. I have collected
Stars from that sky, laid them on ledges,
Rubbed shoulders with storms, the glass protecting.
Possessive, feverish, populous, I
Have plaited birds with their sounds. Today

Is not in time, is another order.
Nostalgia echoes, the early hours
Which were not hours are holding me.

145

I am tied up fast by trails of cards,
The threads of unfinished conversation.
I am a shape, a cube perhaps,
Now being sucked. But apparitions

Install themselves. I did not know
How acutely reliant I could be
On the lean of a card, the look of a toy.
Someone is taking over already.
Bruised by a fleck of dust, I pick
Some papers up and close my eyes

To the stars once fixed for me outside,
Stuff my ears against the insistent
Lovable echoes. I need a conversion,
Change into one who does not own,
Believe my belongings supply no need,
Then am heretic to the bone.

Deaf

Her mind is pushing slowly through the doors
Which others do not think about since they
Toss up their senses like a conjuror's
Five cards or streamers. She must find a way
To catch a tone or pause.

But it is nonsense that the eyes make up
For lack of hearing. Hers, obliquely bright,
Have no exchange with touch or tongue or lip.
Their brown is but a tension, not a sight,
But when the eyelids droop

She hunts and stalks her family. Their names
Come out in questions. Silver deaf-aid is
A mockery, a shaken box of themes
Whose high notes are distorted, dissonance,
As though she spoke her dreams

And asked us for the meaning. Hidden mind,
Muffled behind a face which never has
Tautened to adult enterprise, been lined
With cross-hatched disapprovals, your distress
Is terribly unblind.

Night Worker by Nature

Almost the last thing I shall see,
My morning is near waking time
For others. Factory night-workers
Are yawning at conveyor-belts,
   Newspapers fell off trains

Four hours ago. My lean-to hours,
Shaped small by others, not by me,
Are shuffled books, precluding lamp,
A curtain keeping out the stars.
   No stars, though, when I switch

The light off. One long strip of grey,
Where curtains can't be dragged to meet,
I watch, then hump my back against
Sky coming in to spark my feet,
   Sun-rise, two hours away.

Birds call across my almost-sleep,
Draw drowsy waking into my
Drowsing-asleep. Night-worker, I
Have felt reluctant power keep
   Clocks back but not that sky.

The only chanticleer I know
Runs with the wind, washed by the moon.
Its plumage folds. This cock has no
Voice to attend the day. The sun
   May gild it upon show.

I shall not see. My room takes form –
A Cubist's gathering of things
In muted colours, my last sight,
My dream-connected lingerings,
    My last touch on the night.

An Attempt to Charm Sleep

A certain blue
A very dark one
Navy-blue
Going to school
Get back to colour
A pale blue
Somebody's eyes
Or were they grey
Who was the person
Did they like me
Go back to colour
An intolerant blue
A very deep
Inviting water
Is it a river
Where is it going
Shall I swim
What is its name
Go back to colour
Go back to waking
The spell doesn't work
As I stare at the night
It seems like blue.

The Poem at Times

Summons on the mind,
Seizing and questing, an
Attack, a coming to,
Excitement eased at once,
The found word, and the shine

As if, from water plucked
But never losing light,
Wash of the river still
Yet now on land at last.
The writing's on a spool.

Box-Room

It is empty. Anyone entering hears
The creak of themselves. Boxes once
Held moth-eaten clothes and Teddy Bears.
That was before the going,
The gathering-up for the dance.

It is almost impossible to feel
Untouched by haphazard memory's glance.
Either your own or another's will steal
Into the gala of going,
The drawing-away to dance.

Cancer

Were the others warned of this also
Who saw the fingers flimsy as that disc
Of palatable bread, the over-flow
Of soda-water swallowed with no risk?
They must have seen the slow

Faltering, the body drooping dress
And cardigan. But they had their own ways –
Deafness, the tilted mind, or loneliness.
At first it was an ectoplasmic haze
I saw her through, distress,

Fear of my own, all that I had been told.
Motives don't mean much when uncoffined death
Walks in a woman not aware of cold,
Knowing, however, that each push of breath
Has not the power to hold.

She talked no stoic talk, nor thrived on past
Promise. She did not know I knew she had
The medical prediction and forecast –
A year or maybe two. Below my bed
She lies, but does she rest,

Does the Faith I was told of falter where
She is alone? She only let a hint
Of any creed out with a casual air,
Yes, almost an aside. Acceptance sent
Shivers through me, not her.

Observing

That tree across the way
Has been a magnet to me all this year.
What happens to it is what interests me.
   I've watched a blackbird stay
Glued for a moment, unglue, disappear.
Violence came in April to that tree,
   Made its whole being sway

   Till I was sure it could
Not stand, would snap and in torn fragments lie,
Leaving another entrance for the sky.
   But that frail-seeming wood,
A conifer with intricate small leaves,
Stands under stars now while a new moon conceives
   Itself before the eye.

Celebration of Winter

Any voice is soprano in this air,
Every star is seeding, every tree
Is a sign of belonging or being free,
Of being strong in the Winter atmosphere.
Nobody hesitates here.

150

There are sounds and there are spaces.
Human creatures could have left long ago,
Birds are migrants except
For an owl which woos and lullabies the night.
We are only waiting for snow.
The wind has swept away the brooding Summer,
Or has it taken flight?
Nostalgias are null. Eyes are a taper alight.

And Winter reaches ahead, it stretches, it goes
Further than dark. A fountain is somewhere still.
What voice will come and fill
The emptiness of its no-longer overflows?
Any birth in Winter is hallowed by more
Than Advents or Bethlehems. The seas compose
Themselves perhaps for an Age of Ice, a shore
Where a child lifts a wave, where one gull chose
Not an inland cluster but broken wing and claw.
Any voice is sharpened upon this air
And if the sky sagged there would be more than one star to
    spare.

To Go with a Present

I will risk threats of gazing at the most appetising
Mirrors and turning away with bleakness. I will gather more
    As a geologist than a gardener, stones where fossils may be
        engraved
And give you the completest. This will last and though lacking
    The bounty and exuberance of full Summer flowers
Be quiet as I wish, as I want these words to be. For gratitude

Is an honour conferred and requires always that subtle
Blend of the spontaneous with the studied. With all thanks
    A present should go. You handed over more
Than a dedication. You gave me a portrait and a mood and I
    Am amazed still at the authority of your perception, your
        gentleness.

A Little More

Each minute of a further light
Draws me towards perspective Spring.
I fold the minutes back each night,
   I hear the gossiping

Of birds whose instinct carries time,
A watch tucked in the flourished breast.
It ticks the second they must climb
   Into a narrow nest.

So birds. But I am not thus powered.
Impulse has gone. My measured cells
Of brain and knowledge are too stored,
   And trust to birds and bells.

Yet longer light is fetching me
To hopes I have no reason for.
A further lease of light each day
   Suggests irrational more.

Comfort

Hand closed upon another, warm.
The other, cold, turned round and met
And found a weather made of calm.
So sadness goes, and so regret.

A touch, a magic in the hand.
Not what the fortune-teller sees
Or thinks that she can understand.
This warm hand binds but also frees.

This Is

This is to be unpossessive,
This is a way to earn
A portion of the clasp

Of sun. An eye can glean
The stars. They ride there still,
Are never gathered in.

And by nocturnal sea
A man may rest his dark
Which one wave laps upon.
This is a blessing, this
Awe which is silent, breath
Borne on a flight of wind.

Never Going

We were always going
Further up the beach
Or further down,
However you regard it.
This was always planned
For after siesta
One afternoon,
But we never went.
Why didn't we?

Stopped by the heat?
More than once certainly.
Or was it the familiar walk
Where, even abroad,
We had made landmarks,
Wanted to stick to them,
Streets became personal
With our private names?

How easily then
We dismissed that journey
Thinking, I suppose,
"There will be another time.
Today is all wrong."
I shall not go there,
Not even to that town
Where you could have died.

No, that was elsewhere,
And that intended journey
Is prepared and plotted
For other people's footsteps.
There are no spoors of ours
And I won't go there alone.

A Gentle Command

May we retain
Such scope in which we play and love
That we do not exclude
All those who have no heart to move,
Fearing to spoil or strain,
Towards what is for us both joy and food.

Abandon, then
Secret looks, I charge you, and
This self I need to school
From subtle ways which guard a land
And keep off other men.
This paradox will make us spare and full.

In Itself

The rarity, the root, the flower,
The things themselves, not the abouts,
The magic wand of naming, power
That dreads away the darks, the doubts –

All this and see, a child appears
White as unfootstepped snow and strong
As dissipators of spread fears.
He stands and sings. It is a song

He's thought, a purpose of pure sound.
This child is conjurer, can make
The roots thrill in the frozen ground,
Petals fold up for buds to break.

Gained

The day is not impoverished any more.
The sun came very late but never mind,
The sky has opened like an unwedged door
And for a moment we are all struck blind,
But blind with happiness. Birds' feathers toss
The air aside, regaining all the loss.

The loss of morning which was quietly grey,
Expectant, but what of? We did not know.
Our disappointment had discarded day
Until this early evening with its show
Of caught-up hours, sun's rising, sunset's glow.

Fragment for the Dark

Let it not come near me, let it not
Fold round or over me. One weak hand
Clutches a foot of air, asks the brisk buds
To suffer grey winds, spear through
Fog I feel in me. Give me the magic
To see grounded starlings, their polish
As this threat of all-day night. Mind, mind
In me, make thoughts candles to light me
Out of the furthest reach of possible nights.
Lantern me, stars, if I look up through wet hands,
Show assurance in blurred shining. I have
Put every light in the house on.
May their filaments last till true morning.

My Seasons

I am a kind of Persephone perhaps
Would gladly be underground or asleep in the dark
Winters, would certainly hibernate if I could.

155

I count so many springs since a hint of one
Excites. I have never learnt the way of seasons
Or not of English ones which I ought to know.

If I were Persephone I would be coming and going
Back to the dark, lacking an instinct for
The precise moment when spring has arrived for sure.

I smell the nights, I cast a net of hope
Round a morning sun, I rub my shoulders with shoots,
I challenge the sky to be gentle with the lambs,

Gentle with me also. When the cuckoo gives
Its wooing double call I put out my hands
For feathers to drop from nests. I obey the winds

And let them carry me where they will. I give
All astrology up for a spread of stars
And a sickle moon meaning so many kinds of gold.

Song for the Swifts

The swifts have now returned.
They volley, parry, play with the new light,
Dance under pieces of cloud then, out of sight,
Tease us with the pleasure of their flight,
Become our luxury too. The wind's weight
    Is once again to·be learned,

To be taught to us by each swift.
Melancholies are carried away in the stride
Of the tamed clouds and spring has opened wide
Its windows, these birds assisting. They have defied
Drowning waves, peaks few men have tried
    And they have come to lift

Our minds and natures too.
Envy cowers with so much to be shared,
Love revives as we count up the paired,

Unthinkingly mating birds. Cold winds are repaired
By South the swifts have brought and we are snared
    By joy, know what to do.

    However dark our lands,
Wisdom is in our bloodstream not in brain
Alone and we take instinct on again
Watching these birds and the soon-to-bear-fruit grain,
And what we never thought we could attain
    Falls, the uneaten apple, in our hands.

The Sleep of Birds

We cannot hear the birds sleeping
Under the trees, under the flowers, under the eyes of our watching
And the rustling over of sheets of our unsleeping
Or our final whispers of loving.
How enviable this solemn silence of theirs
Like the quiet of monks tired with their singing hours
And dreaming about the next.
Birds are remote as stars by being silent
And will flash out like stars at their punctual dawn
As the stars are snuffed by the sun.

Does this quiet sleep of birds hide dreams, hide nightmares?
Does the lash of wind and the failing wing and the falling
Out of the air enter their sleep? Let us listen,
Open the window and listen
For a cry of a nightmare to underline the night.
There is no cry, there is only
The one feathered life who's not awake and does not sing
But hoots and holds his own, his own now being
A lordly and humorous comment upon the darkness,
A quiet joke at the changing demands of the moon.

Old People's Nursing Home

The men have ceased to be men, the women, women.
Or so it appears at first.
Here are children dressed for a meal, napkins in collars,
Here are meals from the nursery, here is the nurse.
So it appears to one who is half
Within this house and half outside.
"It will be calm", someone suggested.

And so it seemed at first – tidy and calm
With the weather outside tidy and calm,
The carpets, pressed to the walls, forbidding noise,
No smell of a hospital, no smell at all,
And that was what I longed for first, the scent
Of a hyacinth bypassing sickness and pungent with growth,
Perfume thrust on the wrist and rising in clouds
In circles of foreign summers.

But there was no smell, not even the deathly sick
Odour of death. And then I realized:
Death is shut from this house, the language of death,
The accoutrements of dying.
A ghost would be lively. Ghosts are not allowed here
And neither is talk of birth.

The faces differentiate themselves,
The men half-women, the women half-men
And each entirely children
Except in anger, except in ignorance.
These wrinkled faces know too much, these gnarled
Hands have touched the pulse of love, have known
The family increase and birth's harvesting.

But that was the past and this house has shut out the past
And it dare not face the future:
So it lives in a perilous present that could be cracked
By a broken cup or a laugh.
Cups are unbreakable here,
Jokes are in print too small
And the noisy future, the passionate past are dammed
Partly by deafness, partly
By doctors' decisions and nurses'

Hiding the stuff of life and death away –
Tear-heavy handkerchiefs, the whiff of pain.

And I who carry compassion find it useless,
I who am very young here feel part-guilty,
Part-helpless. Most, out of place.
For my past and future spread throughout my present,
Time is a scheme of light and dark,
"What is the time?" an old woman whispers.
Nobody answers and I,
With a load of compassion to scatter, refuse to tell her
For to do so would set the rainbow over this house,
Of movements and mornings which lead to death, and death
Is an outcast here for a night, for an hour, for how long?

Death of an Old Lady

The wind came up this afternoon and I,
Blown like a feather, shivering into
The small warmth of me, thought "Today you die,
Blown out also, clean gone, the whole of you."
Last night I saw you lie

Sleeping, a little human bag of bone
With pallid skin stretched over it. You were
Alive, heart beating, one flame flickering on.
Then all the usual, human questions, "Where?"
And "Why?" pressed down upon

My three months' love of you. The stormy night
In retrospect seemed part of all of this,
The quiet morning suitable with bright
Still air, a calm much like the fantasies
To which you gave me right

Of entry. There were no farewells for us.
The wind lifts branches now, is snapping small
Twigs and there's a wind both boisterous
And grave, like death which needs no dirge or bells
But happens with no fuss.

Cradle Catholic

The hope and charity may go
A moment but the faith that's you,
You I can't feel and never see,
Yet feed on my identity.
O Christ, can it be ever just
To make a burden out of trust?

Love does. I mean our human love
And you are man but spoken of
As God. To make life simplified
You were a little child who died.
O take my unlove and despair
And what they lack let faith repair.

Michelangelo's First Pietà

Carve a compassion. Older than you are
He lies upon your lap. What can you do
But hold him with a trust you also fear?
    Thus Michelangelo

Saw what a girl may do for gods. O we
Have mercy on this man a woman holds,
God in the grip of our humanity.
    All this the sculptor moulds.

But more. It is a prayer that he is saying
Wordless, except that written on her breast
He writes his name. This girl he is displaying
    Has also brought him rest.

Sufism

This God is a veil over the world but is also shining at us
Through all growth, hides in the detailed veins of a leaf, in the
    dance
Of petals in wind, in the four quartered wind also and in

Each different turn of a wave, each diverse groove in the sand,
    and in
  All eyes, whether of fish or lion or a bold child outstaring
The sun. Let the veil be stripped off, the Sufis say, let God
  Step out of his own inventions. Let us prepare our poems and
    music and
Dervishing dances for his delectation. What we seek is to grow
    to a full
  Maturity. The way is freedom, the means and the only means
    is love.

  So they gathered in groups and chanted, others wrote poems,
    some
Tapped or plucked instruments, and all were preparing a home, a
  Paradise for their creator, one who could span the sky and also
Be caught in the cup of a mountain flower, in the wings of a
    dragon-fly
  Hovering over the water. Let us dance, these seekers, these
    mystics said,
Let us chant for not only in silence is our God at hand, he will
    bound to life
  And sport with and glory in his creation if we
Will play with his games, be serious also with his ways with us
    as he spins
  The world we are on. Let us take it to us like lovers, embrace
    the God we have summoned.

For Edward Thomas

I have looked about for you many times,
Mostly in woods or down quiet roads,
Often in birds whose question-times
Sound like the echo of your moods

When sombre. I've not found you yet
In day sounds or dream-threaded night
You watched through, tired-eyed. I set
Such places by, finding no sight

Of you in this strange hunt. I turn
Back to your words. You do not haunt
Them either. Suddenly I learn
Your art of being reticent,

Of leaving birds, trees, hills alone.
You left no spirit in any place
Or spoors of yours where you had gone.
Yet, though there is no print or trace

Of you, I *see* a different way,
As if your writing were a shine
Upon cool suns, your words the play
Of stars with water, your dark – mine.

Cézanne

What others would see as a foreshadowing of, or
Beginning of Cubism was for you a mathematical problem
    Worked out in sketches and later in paint. Then, where
Does the joy, the always-escaping ecstasy enter, that
    Shiver along the skin, that unique excitement never to be
Sought or even hoped for? Maybe the problems presented by
    Stone and light never seemed like such to you. Maybe

The solution was found and appeared like that fitful achieving
All artists recognize but will not try to explain for they
    Are always moving off, always discarding. So you –
The lesson learnt and, accepted as an intuition – approached
    Other scenes, faces, objects with a new advantage now, though
Analyst as you were, you probably, being ahead of what you had
    Attained, were only after more surfaces to break, more
Appearances to probe, the rainbow to you being
    What a syllogism is to a philosopher, only more so, more so
        since
It leads on, is not sealed off, solves according to the artist nothing
    at all finally, at least for him, above all not for him.

Chinese Poem

It would be an error to suppose
This is impersonal.
True the sky is drained of all but palest
Blue, and true that one cool willow here
Repeats itself in water never rough.

But look more closely, watch the handiwork,
The painter gives himself away in his
Careful calligraphy.
He signs himself in letters which themselves
Are further pictures, miniatures and all
Are upright, at attention.

Here we may gaze at coolness which is worked for.
Monet would have understood how closely
This painter's eye studied the way all water
Is on the move, is never still because
Sun whether dazzling or, as here, concealed,
Coaxes it constantly in serious play.
This eastern painter sent his brushes chasing
To marry elements and keep them linked,
Water and airy light, in unison,
But drawn together by a human touch.

Night Concert at Taormina

(The Greco-Roman Theatre)

The spectacle is changing into sound,
The columns, plucked by song, turn into light,
Two key-boards rise in triumph from the ground
And fill the spaces of a warm good-night.

The century does not matter or the name,
The careful fingers put the stars in place.
Listen, the movements make a kindly claim
And lift the troubled glances from each face.

163

O hush the huge half-circle and recall
The ruined Greeks, the flaunting Romans. Here
Their echoes are drawn back and lightly fall

From keys which open more than heart or mind
As four hands in a moon-warmed theatre
Release our violence and make us kind.

The Ladybird's Story

It was a roadway to me.
So many meeting-places and directions.
It was smooth, polished, sometimes it shook a little
But I did not tumble off.
I heard you say, and it was like a siren,
"A ladybird. Good luck. Perhaps some money."
I did not understand.
Suddenly I was frightened, fearful of falling
Because you lifted your hand.

And then I saw your eyes,
Glassy moons always changing shape,
Sometimes suns in eclipse.
I watched the beak, the peak of your huge nose
And the island of your lips.
I was afraid but you were not. I have
No sting. I do not wound.
I carry a brittle coat. It does not protect.
I thought you would blow me away but superstition
Saved me. You held your hand now in one position,
Gentled me over the veins and arteries.
But it was not I you cared about but money.
You see I have watched you with flies.

The Sparrows' Chorus

How often you forget about us! We are
About all through the year.
Our feathers are drab, beside other birds we appear
Nonentities, no fashion parades for us.
Nobody makes a fuss
Of us and really we don't care,
At least, not too much.
But we are faithful, whatever the weather we stay
Among you. And don't think we're ungrateful for the food
Some of you like to toss.
We need it badly. We can lose half our weight
On an icy night. We depend a lot on you.

Often, we have to admit, we wish we wore
Flamboyant colours. A yellow, a red, a blue.
The robin is lucky and all the tits are too.
But perhaps our smallness is noticeable. Beside
A starling or blackbird we are almost invisible
But don't forget we are here,
Domestic creatures, never flying far.
Just to exist through an English climate is
Remarkable.
It's almost a miracle simply that we are.

The Thrush Confides

The truth about me is I am
One who enjoys life, who feels
Happy most of the time.
Whatever weather may come –
Wind, rain, enormous falls
Of snow – I feel at home
And would like you to feel much the same.

And please don't imagine that I
Am stupid or priggish. I'm not.
I know I'm not handsome, not one
Who people point at and cry

165

"What a very remarkable sight."
I like being left alone
To find worms, look about, feel the sun.

The Fieldmouse's Monologue

Didn't you know how frightened I was when I came
For shelter in your room? I am not tame.
You looked enormous when I saw you first.
I rushed to the hole I had made, took refuge there,
Crouched behind paper you thrust at me, shivered with fear.
I had smelt some chocolate. The kitchen was warm below
And outside there was frost and, one whole night, great snow.

I only guessed you were frightened too when you
Called out loudly, deafeningly to me.
My ears are small but my hearing strong, you see.
You pushed old papers against my hole and so
I had to climb into a drawer. You did not know
That I could run so high. I felt your hand,
Like my world in shadow, shudder across me and
I scuttled away but felt a kind of bond
With you in your huge fear.
Was I the only friend near?

The Hedgehog's Explanation

I move very slowly,
I would like to be friendly,
Yet my prickly back has a look of danger. You might
Suppose I were ready for war or at least a fight
With a cat on the wall, a gather of birds, but no,
My prickles damage nobody, so you

Must be gentle with me, you with your huge shadow,
Your footsteps like claps of thunder,
The terrible touch of your hands.
Listen to me: I am a ball of fear,
Terror is what I know best,

166

What I live with and dream about.
Put out a saucer of milk for me,
Keep me from roads and cars.
If *you* want to look after someone,
Take care of me
And give me at least the pretence I am safe and free.

The Sheep's Confession

I look stupid, much like a dirty heap of snow
The Winter left.
I have nothing to draw your attention, nothing for show,
Except the craft

Which shears me and leaves me looking even more
Unintelligent.
I do not wonder you laugh when you see my bare
Flesh like a tent

Whose guy-ropes broke. But listen, I have one thing
To charm and delight –
The lamb I drop when Winter is turning to Spring.
His coat is white,

Purer than mine and he wears socks of black wool.
He can move
And prance. I am proud of a son so beautiful
And so worthy of love.

The Deers' Request

We are the disappearers.
You may never see us, never,
But if you make your way through a forest
Stepping lightly and gently,
Not plucking or touching or hurting,
You may one day see a shadow

And after the shadow a patch
Of speckled fawn, a glint
Of a horn.
    Those signs mean us.

O chase us never. Don't hurt us.
We who are male carry antlers
Horny, tough, like trees,
But we are terrified creatures,
Are quick to move, are nervous
Of the flutter of birds, of the quietest
Footfall, are frightened of every noise.

If you would learn to be gentle,
To be quiet and happy alone,
Think of our lives in deep forests,
Of those who hunt us and haunt us
And drive us into the ocean.
If you love to play by yourself
Content in that liberty,
Think of us being hunted,
Tell those men to let us be.

Finale for the Animals

Some with cruelty came, sharp-fanged and clawed,
Tore at the air searching for food which, found,
They ate in an instant – new leaves, the tall and small
Flowers. Carnivores were
Worse, hunters of blood, smellers of victims
More miles away than our instruments measure or we
Imagine. Meanwhile the jungle listened and looked.
The parrot kept its beak shut, the slithering snake
Stilled to a coil. The stars were listening, the sun's
Burning paused at the tear and rampage of
A striped or spotted creature. This was the time
Before we were.

Now we have caged and enclosed but not enchanted
Most of these. Now full of power we are not

Gentle with flowers, pull too hard, break the admired
Rose with abandonment. We should know better.

You have heard of the ark and Noah. Most likely it
Was a local event or a myth but remember men ·
Bow down to the myths they create.
Perhaps we were kindest, most gentle,
Most at our best
When we coupled all creatures and launched them forth in an
   ark.
Imagination was gracious then indeed,
Gracious too when we thought up the speeding dove,
Feathery emblem of peace whiter than clouds, its wings
Combing and calming the breakers. The waters stilled.

You have heard now of some of these, learnt of their habits.
Do not haunt zoos too often, do not demand
Affection too often from rabbits or cats or dogs,
Do not tame if taming hurts.
Be grateful for such variety of manners,
For the diverse universe.
Above all respect the smallest of all these creatures
As you are awed by the stars.

Into the Hour

I have come into the hour of a white healing.
Grief's surgery is over and I wear
The scar of my remorse and of my feeling.

I have come into a sudden sunlit hour
When ghosts are scared to corners. I have come
Into the time when grief begins to flower

Into a new love. It had filled my room
Long before I recognized it. Now
I speak its name. Grief finds its good way home.

The apple-blossom's handsome on the bough
And Paradise spreads round. I touch its grass.
I want to celebrate but don't know how.

169

I need not speak though everyone I pass
Stares at me kindly. I would put my hand
Into their hands. Now I have lost my loss

In some way I may later understand.
I hear the singing of the summer grass.
And love, I find, has no considered end,

Nor is it subject to the wilderness
Which follows death. I am not traitor to
A person or a memory. I trace

Behind that love another which is running
Around, ahead. I need not ask its meaning.

Goldfinch

These claws too contain
A bad crop. The goldfinch preys on the blossom
Of apple, that froth and tide of a white
Spring wedding. The neatness, the tailor-made
Touch of his suit bespeaks a harmlessness,
A wish to please that he is stranger to.

Why must we pet the world's destroyers?
I am not speaking of the soft-handed cream-buyers
Or the vendors of fresh liver
To fill the guts of a cat, no, I speak
A contradiction. I praise the pluck of the goldfinch
But I abhor this lamentable *gourmet*
Who plucks from the Eden branch the Eden flower,
Such a bright appearance, such a dandy to the inch.

Forgiveness

Anger, pity, always, most, forgive.
It is the word which we surrender by,
It is the language where we have to live,

For all torn tempers, sulks and brawls at last
Lie down in huge relief as if the world
Paused on its axis. Sorrow does sound best

When whispered near a window which can hold
The full moon or its quarter. Love, I say,
In spite of many hours when I was cold

And obdurate I never meant to stay
Like that or, if I meant to, I can't keep
The anger up. Our storms must draw away,

Their durance is not long. Almost asleep,
I listen now to winds' parley with trees
And feel a kind of comforting so deep

I want to share it. This unpaid-for peace
Possesses me. How much I wish to give
Some back to you, but living's made of these

Moments when every anger comes to grief
And we are rich in right apologies.

Never Such Peace

Never such peace before, never such rest
As when, a gaze away from summer sky
We watched the bleeding and the burning west.
We did not move, we did not even sigh.
Your hand lay on my breast.

And in that centre, as it were, of calm,
It was as if the acts which we had done
Were flared out in the west. The night was warm
And in this personal peace we saw a sun
That burns but does not harm.

Not what you did or what I said's the drift
Now. I remember silence as the light
Seeped down the sky and you and I were left.

It was not day still and it was not night
When we, though sleep-bereft,

Watched an epic sunset, did not move
But stared out at the final act but one.
The elements were copying our love
And dramatising our small union,
And nobody moved off.

A curtain fell, the night's, so slow to come
We did not notice it until the air,
The outer star-packed air flowed through the room.
And when you pointed at one bigger star
Both of us were dumb.

A Weather Spell

Seven times seven and seven again,
Come the wind and come the rain,
Come the snow and come the heat
And come where darts of lightning meet.

Come all weather, come all ways
To join and part or walk a maze.
Come, my love, be light to start.
Let no thunder break your heart.

I will take the elements
And move their dangerous charges. Chance
Is tossed away. I give you choice
And a purpose and a voice.

I will take the dark aside,
Make the furious seas divide,
But most I'll breach the wall of you
Come the heat and come the snow.

I Count the Moments

I count the moments of my mercies up,
I make a list of love and find it full.
I do all this before I fall asleep.

Others examine consciences. I tell
My beads of gracious moments shining still.
I count my good hours and they guide me well

Into a sleepless night. It's when I fill
Pages with what I think I am made for,
A life of writing poems. Then may they heal

The pain of silence for all those who stare
At stars as I do but are helpless to
Make the bright necklace. May I set ajar

The doors of closed minds. Words come and words go
And poetry is pain as well as passion.
But in the large flights of imagination

I see for one crammed second, order so
Explicit that I need no more persuasion.

Love Needs an Elegy

Move over into your own secrecy.
The planet cools. Our bodies lie apart.
I am not part of you, nor you of me,

We have a separate and a wounded heart,
We hear the world, we see the kings go by
And men and children happy from the start.

Why are they so or is it all a lie?
Listen, a wind is rising. I think spring
Is skirmishing today. It feels nearby

Yet we are not affected. I hear wings
And flights. The birds need never heed the clock
Or hear a lonely summons. Such light sings

But we fit nowhere. What is it can break
Hearts while there's good faith still? I do not know;
We keep our promises but stay awake.

If love could be a matter of the will
O this would never be most sadly so.

On Its Own

Never the same and all again.
Well, no same loss will tear me through
Or the same pain grip me if you
Go on your way. I yet shall gain
Knowledge and never wish unknown
The arguments that reach the bone,

The feelings which lay waste the heart.
No tidy place, no, I will have
All the destructiveness of love
If I can know, beyond the hurt,
Happiness waits or partly so
But not like once and long ago.

My world shall be dramatic then,
No repetitions, many acts,
A few hard treaties, broken tracts,
And peace made stronger yet by pain
Accepted but not chosen when
Love is its own and not again.

Death

They did not speak of death
But went round and round the subject deviously.
They were out of breath

With keeping it at bay. When would they see
    That they were burdened with

    Dying like other men?
Immediate mourners know the whole of grief
    When they've seen the dying in pain
And the gradual move toward the end of life.
    O death comes again and again

And starts with the crying child and the doctor's knife.

Spirits

If there are spirits, then they breathe in birds
Tossed by the winds, agile in the frost.
Though the world falls down like a house of cards,
Spirits will soar and in birds put their trust
Who rely on us to feed them as we must

In lengthy winters like the last; it is
Our happy task to keep these fliers going,
To give them nuts and crumbs. When it is snowing
They huddle in the evergreens and press
Their lean, bright breasts upon that lastingness.

But if there are, say, angels, or the Greek
Nymphs, and though it is a fancy to
Speculate, it's thus we like to speak.
Who could believe a nearly dead thing flew
As cold blackbirds so frequently will do?

These are approximations but they touch
As near as men can through the boundaries
Rounding our senses' exploration. Much
Is still mysterious, but man probes and tries
To halt a hope, a fragment where it lies,

A vestige of his dreams. If he lets go
Of it he cannot live. Our dreams express
Acts we daren't do. But let mankind be slow
To lose the impulse of their images.
Releasing them, they'll let so much more go.

A Chorus

Over the surging tides and the mountain kingdoms,
Over the pastoral valleys and the meadows,
Over the cities with their factory darkness,
Over the lands where peace is still a power,
Over all these and all this planet carries
A power broods, invisible monarch, a stranger
To some, but by many trusted. Man's a believer
Until corrupted. This huge trusted power
Is spirit. He moves in the muscle of the world,
In continual creation. He burns the tides, he shines
From the matchless skies. He is the day's surrender.
Recognize him in the eye of the angry tiger,
In the sign of a child stepping at last into sleep,
In whatever touches, graces and confesses,
In hopes fulfilled or forgotten, in promises

Kept, in the resignation of old men –
This spirit, this power, this holder together of space
Is about, is aware, is working in your breathing.
But most he is the need that shows in hunger
And in the tears shed in the lonely fastness.
And in sorrow after anger.

Euthanasia

The law's been passed and I am lying low
Hoping to hide from those who think they are
Kindly, compassionate. My step is slow.
I hurry. Will the executioner
Be watching how I go?

Others about me clearly feel the same.
The deafest one pretends that she can hear.
The blindest hides her white stick while the lame
Attempt to stride. Life has become so dear.
Last time the doctor came,

All who could speak said they felt very well.
Did we imagine he was watching with
A new deep scrutiny? We could not tell.
Each minute now we think the stranger Death
Will take us from each cell

For that is what our little rooms now seem
To be. We are prepared to bear much pain,
Terror attacks us wakeful, every dream
Is now a nightmare. Doctor's due again.
We hold on to the gleam

Of sight, a word to hear. We act, we act,
And doing so we wear our weak selves out.
We said "We want to die" once when we lacked
The chance of it. We wait in fear and doubt.
O life, you are so packed

With possibility. Old age seems good.
The ache, the anguish – we could bear them we
Declare. The ones who pray plead with their God
To turn the murdering ministers away,
But they come softly shod.

Spring Twilight

This is that good hour when
The dying twitterings of several birds
    Speak, but in a lower strain
Of spring wrought of suggestions moving towards
A world of etched trees, all in silhouette
As the pale, drained sky shows the sun has set.

    One window in my room
Is open to the warmth that channels through
    Shafts of coldness. I have come
Into a season and all acts I do
Are steeped in gold, royal authority.
I am the shadow locked into that tree

A dozen yards away.
I am the new moon pencilled on the sky
    And I am my whole yesterday,
But most I am this moment, am held by
Its crystal dome around me. When it's night
I shall be all the scattered stars in sight.

    And as I stare around
My room, it interests me with shadows of
    Ruled, careful lines, a geometry
But also an old exercise of love,
Shaped partly of a spirit quick to take
Colour from climate. When it is daybreak

The moment's clarity will sunder and
I'll take the sun's white wafer on my hand.

Christmas Suite in Five Movements

1   *The Fear*

So simple, very few
Can be so bare, be open to the wide
Dark, the starless night, the day's persistent
Wearing away of time. See, men cast off
Their finery and lay it on the floor,

Here, of a stable. What do they wait for?
Answers to learned questions? No, they have
Been steeped in books and wear the dust of them.

Philosophy breaks all its definitions,
Logic is lost, and here
The Word is silent. This God fears the night,
A child so terrified he asks for us.
God is the cry we thought came from our own
Perpetual sense of loss.
Can God be frightened to be so alone?
Does that child dream the Cross?

2 *The Child*

Blood on a berry,
  Night of frost.
Some make merry.
  Some are lost.

Footsteps crack
  On a pool of ice.
Hope is back.
  This baby lies

Wrapped in rags,
  Is fed by a girl.
O if God begs,
  Then we all hold

Him in our power.
  We catch our breath.
This is the hour
  For the terrible truth,

Terrible, yes,
  But sweet also.
God needs us.
  Now, through snow,

Tomorrow through heat
  We carry him
And hear his heart
  And bring him home.

3 *A Litany*

Mary of solace, take our hope,
Girl untouched, take our hands,
Lady of Heaven, come to our homes,
You bring Heaven down.

Mary of mercy, learn our laws,
Lady of care, take impulse to
Your heart, give us grace,
More than enough
And a relish for
The renewal of love.

Queen of formal gardens, reach our forests,
Girl of the fountains, come into our desert.
Mary of broken hearts, help us to keep
Promises. Lady of wakefulness, take our sleep.
You hold God in your arms and he may weep.

4 The Despair

All night you fought the dream and when you woke
Lay exhausted, blinded by the sun.
How could you face the day which had begun?
As we do, Christ, but worse for you. You broke
Into our history. History drives you on.

Love before this was dust, but it was dust
You took upon yourself. Your empty hands
Have scars upon them. You have made amends
For all wrong acts, for love brought down to lust.
God, the world is crying and man stands

Upon the brink of worse than tragedy.
That was noble. Now there's something more
Than careful scenes and acts. Some men make war
On you and we feel helpless, are not free
To struggle for you. God, we've seen you poor

And cold. Are stars dispensing light that you
Should find the universe turned...can it be
Away from you? No, no, we cannot see
Far or fully. Christ, just born, you go
Back to the blighted, on to the thriving Tree.

5 The Victory

Down to that littleness, down to all that
Crying and hunger, all that tiny flesh
And flickering spirit – down the great stars fall,
Here the huge kings bow.
Here the farmer sees his fragile lambs,
Here the wise man throws his books away.

This manger is the universe's cradle,
This singing mother has the words of truth.

180

Here the ox and ass and sparrow stop,
Here the hopeless man breaks into trust.
God, you have made a victory for the lost.
Give us this daily Bread, this little Host.

Autumn

Fragile, notice that
As autumn starts, a light
Frost crisps up at night
And next day, for a while,
White covers path and lawn.
"Autumn is here, it is,"
Sings the stoical blackbird
But by noon pure gold is tossed
On everything. Leaves fall
As if they meant to rise.
Nothing of nature's lost,
The birth, the blight of things,
The bud, the stretching wings.

Sermon of the Hills
in Tuscany

We are voices but never the voices of mountains,
We have dignity but never condescend,
The good trees burst in flower and fruit upon us,
And the olive prepares its oil and the vineyard loves us;
They speak of us quietly, mostly in the spring.

There are quarries hacked from our many sides,
Oxen who plough out ledges. But the sun,
Ah the sun nests against us in every season's *siesta*.
All are reticent here, almost silent.
But across our valley a little village speaks

And the old and young live their lives in public air.
We are a distance of sky, a channel of water
Entering the silence of men.
So we teach you calm and diffidence but also
Love which sighs from a midnight street for a few,

Love that surrenders day by day at a Mass,
Love that takes the stranger into its calm.
We lean against the sky and all the stars
Are silver flares struck from our many stones.

A Kind of Catalogue

Item, a cloud, and how it changes shape,
Now a pink balloon, then a white shift
From a Victorian doll. The forms won't keep
One pattern long. Item, a flow of wind
Carrying dust and paper, gathering up

Rose petals. Item, a command of sun
Subtly presented on a lifted face,
A shaft of light on leaves, darkness undone
And packed away. Item, limbs moved with grace,
Turning the air aside. Item, my own

Observations, now *Lot This, Lot That*
Ready for an unseen auctioneer.
The bidders are half-conscious choices met
To haggle. Signs are made, sometimes I hear
My whisper bidding for *Lot This, Lot That*.

Over and Over

Over and over they suffer, the gentle creatures,
The frightened deer, the mice in the corn to be gathered,
Over and over we cry, alone or together.
And we weep for a lot we scarcely understand,

Wondering why we are here and what we mean
And why there are huge stars and volcanic eruptions,
Earthquakes, desperate disasters of many kinds.
What is the answer? Is there

One? There are many. Most of us forget
The times when the going sun was a blaze of gold
And the blue hung behind it and we were the whole of awe,
We forget the moments of love and cast out time
And the children who come to us trusting the answers we give
To their difficult and important questions. And there

Are shooting stars and rainbows and broad blue seas.
Surely when we gather the good abou. us
The dark is cancelled out. Mysteries must
Be our way of life. Without them we might
Stop trying to learn and hoping to succeed
In the work we half-choose and giving the love we need.

Heyday

All was a blossom and a bounty then,
A world of learning pulsing with the young
Keen minds at work, quick eyes to speed to eyes,
Libraries of the great to move among
And all those dazzling, wondering young men.

Enough to turn your head. It never did.
I had my flowering too but it came late.
I was surprised into the magic of
Party or ball, the passionate and sweet
Moment of young men moving into love

And moving me, young too. This one would shine
With love of art and read his poetry,
That one was shy and when he first kissed me
It was a child's touch. Vulnerability
Belonged to all of us. I hid in mine.

Only as it went slowly (an eclipse
Would have been kinder) did I realize
How much admired I was, what careful grace
And disguised awkwardness there were. Such eyes
Followed me far, and then the meeting lips.

As the Rooks Are

Alone as the rooks are
In their high, shaking homes in the sky at the mercy of winds,
Alone as the lurking trout or the owl which hoots
Comfortingly. I have a well-crammed mind
And I have deep-down healthy and tough roots

But in this house where I live
In one big room, there is much solitude,
Solitude which can turn to loneliness if
I let it infect me with its darkening mood.
Away from here I have an abundant life,
Friends, love, acclaim and these are good.

And I have imagination
Which can travel me over mountains and rough seas;
I also have the gift of discrimination.
High in a house which looks over many trees
I collect sunsets and stars which are now a passion.
And I wave my hand to thousands of lives like this,
But will open my window in winter for conversation.

The Child's Story

When I was small and they talked about love I laughed
But I ran away and I hid in a tall tree
Or I lay in asparagus beds
But I still listened.
The blue dome sang with the wildest birds
And the new sun sang in the idle noon

But then I heard love, love, rung from the steeples, each belfry,
And I was afraid and I watched the cypress trees
Join the deciduous chestnuts and oaks in a crowd of shadows
And then I shivered and ran and ran to the tall
White house with the green shutters and dark red door
And I cried "Let me in even if you must love me"
And they came and lifted me up and told me the name
Of the near and the far stars,
And so my first love was.

A Bird in the House

It was a yellow voice, a high, shrill treble in the nursery
White always and high, I remember it so,
White cupboard, off-white table, mugs, dolls' faces
And I was four or five. The garden could have been
Miles away. We were taken down to the green
Asparagus beds, the cut lawn, and the smell of it
Comes each summer after rain when white returns. Our bird,
A canary called Peter, sang behind bars. The black and white cat
Curled and snoozed by the fire and danger was far away.

Far away for us. Safety was life and only now do I know
That white walls and lit leaves knocking windows
Are a good prison but always you have
To escape, fly off from love not felt as love,
But our bird died in his yellow feathers. The quick
Cat caught him, tore him through bars when we were out
And I do not remember tears or sadness, I only
Remember the ritual, the warm yellow feathers we put
In a cardboard egg. What a sense of fitness. How far, I know now,
Ritual goes back, egg to egg, birth to burial and we went
Down the garden softly, two in a small procession,
And the high clouds bent down, the sky pulled aside
Its blue curtains. Death was there or else
Where the wise cat had hidden. That day we buried our bird
With a sense of fitness, not knowing death would be hard
Later, dark, without form or purpose.
After my first true grief I wept, was sad, was dark, but today,
Clear of terror and agony,

The yellow bird sings in my mind and I say
That the child is callous but wise, knows the purpose of play.
And the grief of ten years ago
Now has an ancient rite,
A walk down the garden carrying death in an egg
And the sky singing, the trees still waving farewell
When dying was nothing to know.

For my Sister

"I'm too old to play with you any more" –
The words mean laughter now. But did I care?
Your dozen years to my ten did no more
Than make me stubborn in my games. You were

A figure dwindling, lost among real babies,
Pushing prams, a little mother then
And I, when ill, would find you back again
Wheeling me round. Yes, you were everybody's

Nurse when they were broken, worn, afraid
But I was King of cross-roads, theatres, farms,
Vigilant, a lord of what I'd made,
Sometimes the rigid soldier bearing arms,
Sometimes a look-out on all thorough-fares.

"I'm too old...." You do not seem so now,
Seem yourself made perfect, and indeed
Matriarch, grandmother, careful wife,
Queen over sickness, and you come and go
Busy with all that makes a newborn life,
Fast and thorough. I'm the child still slow.

The Circuses

On my first train at seven years old and the word
Circus running through my mind. The energetic
Clowns and sprightly horses and the elephants
Filled the ring and a man in a top-hat

Conducted it all. How precise is the picture
Detailed from annuals and advertisements,
The primary colours dancing in my mind. London was all
The hush of dark around two rings. I had them
By heart and head. The train pulled in and the smoke
Seethed to the roof of Paddington. I noticed
Little. Even the waxworks were a prelude
For circling figures, rigorous patterns the ponies
Stepped to. We came to Oxford Circus and...
Why does the vision vanish? Why have I no record
Of total disappointment? What did I say when London
Shrank to high buses, screams of brakes and everywhere
Hoardings of grown-ups' dreams? So memory
Shields the future, dulls imagination
And no-one can tell me what I said or whether I cried
When the circle dwindled to traffic, the hope held nothing inside.

A Serious Game

A toy oven stood for a tabernacle
And two pencils in egg-cups were candle-sticks,
A toy train on a string was the thurible
And I priest and server murmuring my own gibberish
Meant to be Latin and sounding so to my ears.
Day after day long, morning and afternoon
I mumbled the old words, sent up imagined smoke
And in my nostrils the real incense smelt to me always
Sweetly of Sunday and Benediction.

I was alone but not lonely in those untimed days,
Of no hours but my own religious ones
With paper discs for the Host. Over and over
I mumbled the good magic, at times would rope in a friend.
Once a Presbyterian school friend had a bad conscience
And would not play my Popish plots, would not bow or pray
And I let her go with scorn on my face and few words, then on
And on I went, never tired of the growing ritual,
Sure of a God in the clouds, sure of things under veils,
Somehow aware of the holy transformation,
Bread into Body, invisible water to unseen blood.

Night after night I dreamt of the morrow's Mass,
Prayer rising up and up to the fragrant stars
And in my hands the story of man's transformings
With no cold Creeds or Bible or bidding prayers,
But what learned men have argued throughout the ages
There in the shining box lay always before me,
And swung on my thurible censing.

A Sky in Childhood

No Sacrament thereafter,
No blaze of blue in a Southern sky,
No Italy of the heart
Would ever gainsay or sunder that good evening
I wandered in a garden of evergreens.
Near summer it must have been
And the moon had squandered her light or the stars had doubled
Each other, so there was no Great Bear any more,
No Milky Way,
But only diamonds on receding velvet,
Lights twinkling, showing me uncounted facets
And a sense in me of awe and wonder I
Had not grown up into or marred but was,
As it seems now, ready there for the sky to find me,
There, had I known it, glad to find myself
And awe overtaking me that only later
Looked back upon would be untarnished marvel
Over a summer night, over my own ten years.

Love-Story

We escaped ourselves by escaping into each other
And even at the time I was reminded of walking on high cliffs
Facing Lundy when I was twelve or thirteen.
The sea below elevated me,
I smelt the pure drench of salt,
The iodine rock-pools

And where I walked ripe hedge-rows
Blew their blackberry scent at me.
And so in this rich, at first, acquaintance with it
Passion was a pause, then a plunge, a long look down, and then
High up to the appearing moon from behind turbulent clouds.
As day fell and the keen chill of twilight took me
I was entering an experience beyond my years,
Tapping old rocks whose names I did not know,
Noting the briar tangles and hearing hidden birds
As later I heard the remote cry of my own amazement,
Explorations self-revealing and temporary
Not a disappointment but a certainty
That there were further explorings and excavations.

So the child on the cliff raised above language and knowledge
Was fulfilled in a later revelation
Shown fitfully only, promising so much,
Sharp, bare, then gone like the southern fall of night,
Dark, cool, and mysterious, stared at by the unacknowledged
    stars.

The Last

Last among the loners,
Last of matters which insinuate
Themselves into your way of life and heart,
Is this lesson which a child resists,
Will not pursue, sure that its Heaven holds
Many saints, sure that there always is
Justice, a garden planted for ripe summer,
Summer the healer, known best of the four
Seasons when childhood is the driving force.

I remembered well
Anger which I could not rein or would not,
Then all the world of strict apologies
And the embarrassment of full forgiveness.
I ran away, I hid, I would not hear
"I have forgotten what you did." I hadn't,
My kingdom was the rule of a dictator
And I was king, of course.

189

But the lesson of injustice won't
Be held away or run from. It comes with
Lap-dog words, like "It's inevitable",
Or "You must just get used to it". I wouldn't
And find it hard today.
And so I will back up the child in temper,
The absolute refusal to believe
Betrayals can't be broken. I know well
That God above the clouds who taught there was
Punishment and reward and nothing else,
Not this drab, fawning, cringing thing injustice.
Even today I find betrayal hard
Not to forgive but to believe exists.

A Class-Room

The day was wide and that whole room was wide,
The sun slanting across the desks, the dust
Of chalk rising. I was listening
As if for the first time,
As if I'd never heard our tongue before,
As if a music came alive for me.
And so it did upon the lift of language,
A battle poem, *Lepanto*. In my blood
The high call stirred and brimmed.
I was possessed yet coming for the first
Time into my own
Country of green and sunlight,
Place of harvest and waiting
Where the corn would never all be garnered but
Leave in the sun always at least one swathe.
So from a battle I learnt this healing peace,
Language a spell over the hungry dreams,
A password and a key. That day is still
Locked in my mind. When poetry is spoken
That door is opened and the light is shed,
The gold of language tongued and minted fresh.
And later I began to use my words,
Stared into verse within that class-room and
Was called at last only by kind inquiry

"How old are you?" "Thirteen"
"You are a thinker". More than thought it was
That caught me up excited, charged and changed,
Made ready for the next fine spell of words,
Locked into language with a golden key.

A Time Ago

I shall never live them down, never tumble over
The bad times and the good for they have shaped me,
Firm under English sun, loving the green
Of early spring and green tips, spikes and blue-bells
And soon the primrose
Returning over and over, every year.
And now I turn back and unroll the coloured years
Till six years' old is the sound of a sudden clapper
And I am steady above the almost summer,
The overall shaking and quaking of wasps and livestock.
I was out with a man with a ferret. It sticks in the mind.
Was it a dream? Was it
A wish becoming a daytime meditation,
Part of my story and current with me now?

It does not matter. Time is a truant to me
And I am my own imagination waking
And the seaside days I still have photographs of,
The feel of sand between my toes, the happy
Fear of the brief waves as they floated my bucket.
And the feather-bed in the boarding-house which we quarrelled
Over to have the first leap on that mattress,
The tickle of feathers turning anger to laughter
And the roses on the wall-paper real enough
As the sea was real, and the ships
Coming in but never to our break-water.
A good thing too, for I have sought them since
Like words relished and found in another language,
A sequence of ship-words, cadences of the ocean
And the frivolous clouds trailing away from the solemn
Sun that shows up every fustian music
And bruises my poems with the brush of harsh endeavour.

The Inheritors

They will fail always in the end – the appropriate garden,
The august, sad music pointing to older griefs,
The cities heavy with history, only at ease
When west winds shake the determined cypresses,
When the choir-boys hold the air with inhuman singing.
These so obvious alternatives to loss
Will always fail. Mythology is better, will point you
To the old stories of Diana and Eurydice,

The sweet and melancholy moments when the gods
Ape our behaviour and step from their sacred groves
Into towns of turmoil, "Where is grief to be lost?" you ask
"Or at least turned into useful fables, the kind
Your children in the fever of first love
Will turn to and appropriate as models?"
How kind and simple seem those first emotions,
Untouched by all the posturing of irony,
Held in the eye and clear before the day,
Standing in their own sufficiency.

For the rest there is only the dignity of the present
Sliding away into the bookish past
While we eye the future through dazzling sunsets or starlight,
Our loss neither belittled nor magnified
But seen in its true form terribly frightened or bewildered,
While our children play the game of first betrayal,
Sure of the ease and luxury of first love
With time's finger only sketching the sun's behaviour.
They were ourselves once long ago, so how
Could we indeed bear to disillusion them?

Elegy in Spring

Even in spring I see an elegy,
A long recall, a cherishing the past.
Easter was early, long before each tree
Was noisy with the nesting habits of
A thrush, a blackbird. Why should death stalk me,

192

The sudden taking and this constant black
Apparel of this planet? I don't know
Except that one great grief comes back to mind
And why should that be so?

The dead rise up with one large Death and I
See it tall, its shadow still stretched far.
Easter's for life abundant, eager care,
A light that climbs, but down
Descends upon this ineffectual care
And begs an elegy.

Friday

We nailed the hands long ago,
Wove the thorns, took up the scourge and shouted
For excitement's sake, we stood at the dusty edge
Of the pebbled path and watched the extreme of pain.

But one or two prayed, one or two
Were silent, shocked, stood back
And remembered remnants of words, a new vision.
The cross is up with its crying victim, the clouds
Cover the sun, we learn a new way to lose
What we did not know we had
Until this bleak and sacrificial day,
Until we turned from our bad
Past and knelt and cried out our dismay,
The dice still clicking, the voices dying away.

In April

This is a time for beginning and forgiving,
Lent and April – how their honour shines,
How they ask a change in all our living

Now where the earth shows such propitious signs,
The bursting blossom, and the birds who sing
As if no winter happened. There are lines

Upon my face, the show of lingering
Sadness and grief; I stand aside from all
This ceremonious joy. The birds who wing

In widening circles must like all things fall
But for this moment seem eternal. I
Have no words, no sign, and no fit call.

Disillusion is a way to die.
I wear the dark of it now like a shawl.

Worth

Summer disposes of us. We are not
Ripe for such disclosures, seldom can
Live up to so much magnanimity
Of growing things. The fountains play and sport
With clustered light. We are such broken men,
Baleful with our eccentricity.

When were we worthy of the ground we tread?
When grateful that we are a presence in
A world we prune and wound? Some say there was
A pristine time with men a noble breed.
When did that end and how did it begin?
If we knew that we would be dressed in grace.

Only our impatience can become
Our walking here and seldom staying still.
Only our wonder lights the world for us
And our descendants. Is this globe a home?
Is it at the mercy of our will?

A Forgetting

Only a sky,
Only a star,
Only a cry
Of chanticleer.

194

Only a day
After the dawn,
No words to say,
The sky comes down,

Only for now,
Soon to be gone.
But we don't know how
Sun will have shone

When it reaches us
And we reach for it.
O, we need grace
From an infinite

God we forget
Too often. He
Takes our defeat
And sets us free.

Let Summer Thrive

Let me be out and let the world do well
With this successful summer. Why should I
Ask it to fit my mood, be winter till
The blue has gone and there is charcoal sky?

Let me let be and enter what lies there
Beyond my shadow. It can do no harm,
I feel a sudden breeze lift up my hair,
Then it subsides and everything is warm.

My purposes are profitless, I'll choose
But, choosing, can I act? Such calm I'd be
Were there no dark and nothing left to lose.

I am the black theme of my history
But summer tells another story. Loss
Batters me yet in storms of memory.

A Kind of Magnet

I came upon a kind of magnet-pull
But where's the metal? I became aware
Not of self, that feuding miscreant,
Invalid sufferer. No, now to the full
I feel the planet cruising through the air
And light's the one important element.

Let mystics climb their ladders to the dark
And wrangle with a Satan's greedy throng.
Let holy people hasten to their work.
There is a star that surely sings a song,
Make no mistake the moon has made its mark

More than in several shapes night after night,
Stars form and group. And is this casual?
What is the power behind the element
Of light? What makes me ask the stars to fill
The air with a new version of Plain-Chant?

Falling

Falling leaves in summer, willows weeping
Into any river, drowned twice over,
The real and the reflected swans go by
Slid by someone's hand it seems.
                          Light's falling
From sun at five o'clock,
                          some small fish darted
By to some end of their own.
                          All slithered then
As the sun slid slowly down the sky.
A day was falling unobtrusively,
Night would fall. How words can tease each other.
Willows gaining dignity at dusk,
And later light from stars,
                          their long stares falling.

Sundowning

It is a Moses rush of light behind
My back and I am scalded in the sheen.
Light-headed sun balances but looks
Ready to fall like my high piles of books,
The sun's as prodigal as it's not been
All day and now there is no puff of wind,

No sound of bird or foot. I hold my breath
And watch my page take fire. It fascinates
And claims my watching, yet I can't stay here,
Errands await. I step out through the air
Gold as the sun now on the heavy slates,
How the sun revels in this earth beneath

Its power and dignity. I feel I must
Record its mood, look to the sun-dial now,
Blow dust from ornaments and hold this hour
Somehow in my own intrinsic power.
I seem to do this though I don't know how.
Night will come softly as a tranquil ghost.

Into the Clouds

I have walked into the clouds where light
Hides and I see little room ahead.
I have crouched in dark left by midnight
And I have wondered at what saints have said
        About the patient sight

Of implications of importance to
The host of men, the lingerers in shade,
And I decide that all mankind is made
Of time that mostly proves he is undue
        For the good words said

By masters of the moment that is held,
By hope and patience with the long unsure
Purposes. Perhaps we should be bold

With clouds high up and, downward, the obscure
Cold places of the world.

Dare I dare what all the wise men told
In the deep past half covered up in cloud?
I would attach a purpose to the world
But some unfocussed fear keeps me in cold
And in the rootless moods

Which add to dark. But spring is almost here
And air is opening for songs and breeze.
In seasons' patient repetitions there
Are hintings of a life without a lease.
Why should this coax out fear?

Endings

Endings
And all our attempts to fob them off, to stay
The tide's impulse, wind's pressure and the hard
Demands of senses, but the pollen flies,
Birds brood on South, but hearts cannot migrate
Or not until love dies.

Proceedings
When space fits time. The lucid lily, full
Rose stand up and gardens are intentions
To make at least one thing whole, ardent, good,
But we who are our impulses forget
Even our best hopes, jostled by conventions
Until the last regret.

Ballad of War

Brutal and vigilant the watchers were,
Pale and lean and disciplined to hate.
They taught us fear because they knew white fear
So well. They stood as sentries at the gate.

Gate of the morning and the dawn's endeavour,
Gate of the mind with fantasies and war,
Gate of sickness and unconquered fever,
Yet haven't we known all such gates before?

The gate of birth and then the broken cord,
The gate of love and holding back from fear,
The gate of language and the golden word
Which speaking makes the lustre disappear?

Who are the watchers? Why won't you reply?
Is the world sick? You turn away in dread.
What are those shadows widening the sky?
Where are the stars and is the new moon dead?

Clarify

Clarify me, please,
God of the galaxies,
Make me a meteor,
Or else a metaphor

So lively that it grows
Beyond its likeness and
Stands on its own, a land
That nobody can lose.

God, give me liberty
But not so much that I
See you on Calvary,
Nailed to the wood by me.

Seasonal Reverie

And the afternoon engages itself with light,
Yolk of egg is the colour of crocuses,
Small purple candles the rest,
And the naked trees are putting on a look
Of almost-green. The days draw out, the sun

Flirts with clouds. This is a good time.
Birds are lively. Sparrows leap and spread,
Then gather in huddles again, made one by a drove
Of starlings, pushful, unhappily-feathered birds,
Though in the right light you can see a rainbow shining
Such as you see on puddles containing oil.
So now is a time for observing every hint
Of preparation. Easter is early this year.
My blood is moving fast, my heart exults
With these becomings and these benedictions.

Nothing

We are nothing, we are
A dream in a cosmic mind,
We are a solitude, an emptiness,
We only exist in others' thought, we grow
In fitful seasons, yet we leave our marks,
Our scratches on dark walls, our prints, our spoors,
Our persecuting wars,
Gentle spirits trust that they are made
Over and over, freshly every day,
Beasts die everywhere.
Over the sun clouds cross and change
In threadbare dark processions.
Insects move and men like insects. Why
Are we set here, frightened of our reflections,
Living in fear yet desperate not to die?

Missed Chances

Preludes and dawns, those spare awakenings
Gone before listened to, how we miss such
Arrays of opportunities. As sun lifts up
Its wings and birds tune their large orchestra,
We are invited out of sleep, called to
Take part, share all such daily, sweet beginnings.

Dramas of dreams rise up, the haze of them
Dries in the sun and the awakened mind.
The spirit's opportunities see flights
We seldom heed. Good moments of regret
Vanish in our wanton rummagings,
O bold designs, O short disparaged nights.

Remembering

Do you remember that dark
Wood where we walked in a heat-wave to find some cool?
You must, I think, since all the trees bowed down
And all the shadows made cool shapes for us.
It was unforgettable, for me, because
Our talk was one with the air and the air washed
Over our hands. Between the different, trees,
A few patches and openings let in light.
We were talking of knowledge and wisdom. Now and then we
Fell into silence deep and filled with what
We had said and we meditated on it and when
We started to speak again there were fewer shapes
Of light and shadows. Had we really been
Talking and staying silent so long? I think
We proved the relativity of time,
And the spirit's power and the great sun going down
Made life seem easier, wisdom longer. I hope
We shall go again though nothing will be the same.
Would we want it to be?

Years Ago

It was what we did not do that I remember,
Places with no markers left by us,
All of a summer, meeting every day,
A memorable summer of hot days,
Day after day of them, evening after evening.
Sometimes we would laze

Upon the river-bank, just touching hands
Or stroking one another's arms with grasses.
Swans floated by seeming to assert
Their dignity. But we too had our own
Decorum in the small-change of first love.

Nothing was elegiac or nostalgic,
We threw time in the river as we threw
Breadcrumbs to an inquisitive duck, and so
Day entered evening with a sweeping gesture,
Idly we talked of food and where to go.

This is the love that I knew long ago.
Before possession, passion, and betrayal.

Tell Me

Tell me where you go
When you look faraway.
I find I am too slow

To catch your mood. I hear
The slow and far-off sea
And waves that beat a shore

That could be trying to
Call us toward our end,
Make us hurry through

This little space of dark.
Yet love can stretch it wide.
Each life means so much work.

You are my wealth, my pride.
The good side of me, see
That you stay by my side

Two roots of one great tree.

A Death Alive

This is a grief I never thought to have.
Ten years ago I learnt the grief of death.
For days I could not speak and all belief,
Trust and the like died with my then-dead love,
His sudden end of life.

Time was too present, memory was shame
And guilt and dark reproach. The years have passed
And I have learnt of love and do not blame
Myself again. I thought grief could not last
But now it's back, the same

Ice in the blood, the wrestle in the night.
My life means grief. No other word will fit
This disillusionment, this loss of light.
Friendship has foundered now upon my life.
I thought your image bright,

Yourself an act of grace. Your letter shows
You drawing to the distance, bringing shock
With wounding words. You are the shape of loss.
You are abroad for days. When you come back
Will all be as it was

Once? Will all that glowing joy, those long,
Excited conversations be the past?
I thought the love between us was so strong
It seemed a starlight purpose made to last.
O break this grieving song.

Bitter Fruit

How many tastes are there of bitter fruit?
How many little poisonings? Can you
Tell me? You so rich once in my thought?
I am afraid of you and this came true
Upon the day I caught

You out in lies, I had not pressed to find
A cause for jealousy. You gave it me
Or rather lack of trust that fills the mind
With darkness. What then will our future be?
  Once it was designed

For and out of happiness. Can trust
Ever be retrieved? We can forgive
Anything but that, it makes us lost.
There is a noon-day sun that mocks at grief
  Before we turn to dust.

Yes, there are many deaths but this today
Seems the worst I've ever known. You are
Distant in fact and distant in a way
You were not till you broke my trust, taught fear
  Darker than I can say.

Growing Ahead

The full and flush of you has gone. I see
Nerves quivering beneath your eyes, a dread
Of something in your mind and not elsewhere.
Then you are troubled by your memory,
"What day is this?" "What time is it?" you say.
Tell me of cross-purposes that led

You into fraught uncertainty. I thought
That growing old would still the nerves and make
Untroubled vagueness maybe but, instead,
Along wild paths you go where I'm not led.
Selfishly I'm hurt that you can take
Paths leading from me. Will you let me break

Into this different world to which you've gone
Reluctantly? You do not ask me and
This "I" insists that I wish I could run
Ahead and show you rise and set of sun,
And then walk back and guide your faltering hand.

Love is a storm so often but there must
Be some still centre. Had you reached it then
Before I understood? Could you not trust
My own brash habits? Are you really lost
To me? And must I let you go again,
Neither companion, shadow or a ghost?

Shall All the Loves

Shall all the loves I knew then come to this
End unprepared for, suddenness within,
And the full memory of a sudden kiss

Scald, turn to ash and slowly then begin
Questions and pain, and anger, worst of all?
Yet though I rave and toss I think of when

All might return, spring hang her lendings full
Of sunlight out and push back winter. Yes,
Hope brims in me even when grey clouds fall,

And reason tells me that you don't mean this,
That there's a happy purpose or some lack
That's not your fault. In dark parenthesis

I stand until I have your answers back.

Awake in the Siesta

Rumours of winds and dusty afternoons,
Others' siesta, I stay wideawake,
The only conscious one here. All cats sleep
Upon their shadows. Hot against the walls
Leaves and butterflies lick the crumbling stone.
Here was I, all by myself and happy,
Content in a country truly my first home.
So Tuscany about six years ago,

In a small town never sought out by tourists,
Nothing important, no mosaics and only
One small church not worth the sight-seer's inspection.
The view from my window was peerless, the shutters wide.
Everything I could possess but no possession.
I laid myself open to the atmosphere,
Dipped my hands in water.
                                        Tuscany
You are a sweetness in my nostrils still,
A view I'd never trade, and, every morning
The promising haze and the emerging hills.

Rome – A Quarter of a Century Ago

I was in Rome twenty-six years ago
        Almost to the day,
All the nostalgia which I used to know
        Shows like fountains which play
Up and down to the basin underneath,
        Rome in her panoply

Of worldly beauty catches at the breath
        But she can be austere.
I knew the honied passion of man's death,
        Had found it everywhere,
But there were elusive spirits, essence of prayer
        Almost anywhere.

Feeling's equivocal with me, I can see
        Rome in my mind. I'm sure
That I shaped no deception, no travesty.
        I learned her disciplined law
And her demands were always sweet to bear,
        What am I wanting for?

Why don't I go back? Why am I afraid
        Of disillusionment there?
Passionate probity, my secret will
        Will come into their own.
The remnants of those months stir in me still.
        Rome wears her laurel crown

And my praises of her sound from every hill,
In their tones I used to drown

In a joy I knew authentic at the time,
A wish to understand prayer.
Up to the top of St Peter's dome I would climb
And wander everywhere
In this city of bulk and fury, song and rhyme,
And the casting out of fear.

Memories of Rome

Balanced here between the sky and street
I am awake when others lie in dreams
Unknown at night. Now I absorb the heat
And walk out slowly where the honeycombs
Of scents rise from the dust. The hour is meet
For wandering. A hint of fountains comes

Defying distance. No-one is about
Except a weary dog. I am alone
As I sit down and take my papers out,
Wait at a table, gladly on my own.
Buildings dissolve and all things call in doubt
The possibility of brick and stone.

The haze lifts slowly and the sun begins
To lower itself. The shutters are put up,
Voices start but scarcely can convince
That they can spring from flesh, but then the deep
Tones of bells draw everyone from sleep.
Such afternoons I've lived again long since.

And so the actual South exists for me
In a dozen ways but mostly it
Comes back in Northern winters stealthily,
Bearing all the attributes of heat.
In empty streets in England still I see
In waking dreams how North and South can meet.

The Way of Words and Language

When you are lost
Even near home, when you feel
The tide turning, a strange sea under you
And you are a pale, rubbed pebble, a sea ghost,

When you have lost
All the high-ways and every dimming sign-post
And the sea is far away and the moon hidden
And your watch has stopped and you have no compass
And feel to yourself like a ghost,

All this later will seem your best
Time for there will be future and memory and the tossed
Tide. Morning will come up and you will open your eyes
And see in the mirror a ghost.

But day will take you and the dawn uncover
The ribbed sand foot by foot and the first light
Will stretch over the grey water and you will know
It is no longer night

But still a time of silence and light like a shielded lamp.
Then you will shake off dreams and recover
What you know is yourself still but changed
And the new sun will come up and pass over
Your hands, your arms, your face and you will discover
A world that the night has re-arranged.

Let this time be. Let the present stay. Do not
Look back. Do not look forward. Let thought
Idle from dream into daylight, and watch, then, the coast
Climb out to dark, to grey, and then to chalk-white
Cliffs till the grey sea goes blue
And then indeed you

Are found and safe at last
And all your thought will grow
And you will unreel it, a silk thread, a long-
Travelling, moving-everywhere line
And it will gradually, as you relax it, become a song
And you will not say "That is mine".

208

A Performance of Henry V at Stratford-upon-Avon

Nature teaches us our tongue again
And the swift sentences came pat. I came
Into cool night rescued from rainy dawn.
And I seethed with language – Henry at
Harfleur and Agincourt came apt for war
In Ireland and the Middle East. Here was
The riddling and right tongue, the feeling words
Solid and dutiful. Aspiring hope
Met purpose in "advantages" and "He
That fights with me today shall be my brother."
Say this is patriotic, out of date.
But you are wrong. It never is too late

For nights of stars and feet that move to an
Iambic measure; all who clapped were linked,
The theatre is our treasury and too,
Our study, school-room, house where mercy is

Dispensed with justice. Shakespeare has the mood
And draws the music from the dullest heart.
This is our birthright, speeches for the dumb
And unaccomplished. Henry has the words
For grief and we learn how to tell of death
With dignity. "All was as cold" she said
"As any stone" and so, we who lacked scope
For big or little deaths, increase, grow up
To purposes and means to face events
Of cruelty, stupidity. I walked
Fast under stars. The Avon wandered on
"Tomorrow and tomorrow". Words aren't worn
Out in this place but can renew our tongue,
Flesh out our feeling, make us apt for life.

Song of Time

Deliver time and let it go
Under wild clouds and passive moon.
Once it was fast, now it is slow.

I loose my hours beneath the sun,
Brisk minutes ebb and flow.

Time is elemental, all
We make in speech and action, yet
Time itself can have a fall
When heart and mind have no regret
And love is how you feel.

O let us dance with time and turn
It to a friend, a willing one.
In time we grow, through time we learn
The visitations of the sun
And ardour of the moon.

Time is not clocks but moves within
The discourse of the learned heart,
It is the way our lives begin.
O leaving time behind's an art
Ahead and now and then.

Dawn Not Yet

Dawn not yet and the night still holding sleepers
Closed in dreams, clams in shelter, a hiding
Of half the world and men turned back into

Primaeval matter. A closed world only tides
Ruminate over. Here men could be fossils
Embedded in strata, all to be discovered

By morning, skilful archaeologist
Cutting down carefully, drawing up debris
Of centuries but also precious gems,

Ivory figurines, kings' hoards. We are shown
Riches the sun at last gives shape and glint to
Sun the explorer, sun the diver too.

The sea is quiet. No bells from church and harbour,
Slow off-white sky. A healing time, right peace
Where monks sing hours somewhere, where small waves settle

As if to hush before the general sleep.
As if to hold the waking worries back
Sea-gulls are swinging softly through the sky,

Almost six and light is spreading now,
Soon the many waking, soon the powers
We cannot handle will make their demands

But now is silence, stillness everywhere
And the good night still holds us in its hands.

Frail Bone

Recall the frail bone,
Anatomy where is lodged
Or so we like to express it
Soul, spirit, mind.
Any sea can drown
Or waterfall distress
This pitiful, easily wounded
In every sense, small being.

But we think we are giants,
Fabulous spirits, a people
Plying time to a curtain
To keep off time, to shed
Shadows we can handle
And alter. With sunset
We become our own nocturnes,
Speak aloud to the stars,
Engage the implacable moon
With our fierce endeavours of power.

But we are falling sand
Through the hour-glass of the planet,
Blown through the universe,

And yet that dust delivers
Defiant speech to the last,
Anomalous oratory.

Dust

We are made of dust, we are
Flying on every wind,
Blown to the back of the earth,
Stormed at, broken, defiled.
We are people of dust
But dust with a living mind.

Dust with a spirit, grace
Goes to the end of the earth,
Follows the dark act, the thought
Lying, wounding, distraught,
We are dust from our birth
But in that dust is wrought

A place for visions, a hope
That reaches beyond the stars,
Conjures and pauses the seas,
Dust discovers our own
Proud, torn destinies.
Yes, we are dust to the bone.

Water Music

What I looked for was a place where water
Flowed continually. It could come
In rapids, over rocks in great falls and
Arrive at stillness far below. I watched
The hidden power. And then I went to rivers,
The source and mouth, the place where estuaries
Were the last, slow-moving waters and
The sea lay not far off continually

Making her music,
Loud gulls interrupting.
At first I only listened to her music,
Slow movements first, the held-back waves
With all their force to rear and roar and stretch
Over the waiting sand. Sea music is
What quiets my spirit. I would like my death
To come as rivers turn, as sea commands.
Let my last journey be to sounds of water.

Precursors

Passages of music, a violin's slow pace, a picture
Recording the sunset but telling more, stating
  History's alarm and hurry. I watched as a child the slow
Leaves turning and taking the sun, and the autumn bonfires,
  The whips of wind blowing a landscape away.
Always it was the half-seen, the just-heard which enthralled –
  My nurse pulling her white dress off in the moonlight,
My sister pushing me in a doll's pram as I recovered
  From a slow illness. There is a library somewhere surely of
Pictures piled waiting for a hand to lift them,
  Books with long markers in them. This is the world
Once ahead of me, now behind me, and yet
  I am waiting still to record some of the themes
Of the music heard before I understood it,
  The books read to me long before I could read
And with me tantalisingly near. So I have come
  To believe that poetry is a restoration
Or else an accompaniment to what is lost
  But half-remembered. Today it is autumn outside
And as the sun reddens the whole landscape
  And a smell of bonfires haunts me, a tune begins
To sing in my mind. It has no words as yet
  And a life and a half would probably be too short
To set the music down with appropriate words,
  Record a season completely, words before death.